the

anthology

Edited by
Glenn Carmichael
&
Sara-Jane Arbury

Published by:

PIMP$ of the ALPHAB£T PRESS

130c Lower Cheltenham Place
Montpelier
Bristol   BS6   5LF

British Library Cataloguing in Publication Data.
A catalogue record for this book is available from the British Library.

First Edition
Published 1998

ISBN: 0-9526432-4-3

Printed & bound in Ireland by:
Colour Books Ltd.
Unit 105 Baldoyle Industrial Estate, Baldoyle, Dublin 13.

LET'S SLAM!

CONTENTS

A BRIEF HISTORY

Slamming is competitive poetry, where the poets' performances are scored by the audience.

Slamming began in August 1986 at the Green Mill Lounge, Chicago; invented by Marc Smith, a construction worker/poet.

The Bristol Poetry Slam

Glenn Carmichael had been involved in the British performance poetry scene since 1988 and co-founded the Hard Edge Club in London's Soho. Arriving in Bristol in 1993, he was keen to energise poetry in the area. In the summer of 1994, Glenn witnessed his first slam in the Poetry and Words Tent at Glastonbury Festival and realised that Slam was the medium to take poetry into the 21st Century. He visited America to see slamming stateside, before returning to host the first Bristol Poetry Slam on Tuesday 13th December 1994. Glenn's co-host was Glastonbury compere Lesley Anne Rose. It was a massive success.

After a few venue changes, The Bristol Poetry Slam settled at the Bristol Flyer on the last Tuesday of each month. In June 1995, which saw the first InterCity Slam (against London), Lesley Anne Rose left Bristol to go to university. She was succeeded by Claire Williamson. Claire had performed at the first Bristol Poetry Slam and had followed its progress with enthusiasm.

The new alliance saw the beginning of Exhibition Slams, workshops in schools, promotion of the most popular poets on the circuit today and recognition of Bristol as a leading force in British Performance Poetry. By April 1997, The Bristol Poetry Slam had outgrown the capacity of the Bristol Flyer and was invited to Jesters, a club ideally suited to showcasing the spoken word.

The popularity of Slam now firmly established, Glenn and Claire felt confident enough to organise a UK Poetry Slam Championship. They drafted in Francine Russell (who has always been the welcoming face at the door of the monthly slams) to be their fundraiser. Over the following year, they networked with poets from towns and cities throughout the UK and The UK Poetry Slam Championships 1997 took place in Bristol at Watershed Media Centre, on Saturday 22nd November. It was a sell-out event with 14 teams taking part. Celebrity judges were performance poets John Cooper Clarke, Pink Sly, Patience Agbabi plus Alison B, editor of *strangefish*, and Robin Hague, station manager of GWR fm. Prizes were donated by Faber & Faber and Murray Lachlan Young. The event attracted much media coverage, bringing performance poetry to the attention of a wider and more diverse audience.

A Typical Night at The Bristol Poetry Slam

The evening begins with groovy tunes spun by The Monarch of Mono, Mr Steve Rice, while the audience mingles. At 8.30pm, Glenn and Claire take to the stage and the proceedings begin in their inimitable style of post game show chic. Glenn gives a brief history of Slam, Claire describes how the evening will run, then the disclaimer:

"We disdain/ competition and its ally war/ and are fighting for our very lives/ and the spinning/ of poetry's cocoon of action/ in your dailiness. We refuse/ to meld the contradictions but/ will always walk the razor's edge/ for your love. Remember: The best poet/ always loses."*

At this point The Slam begins.

1: The Heats

The poets' names are drawn from a hat by audience members, in heats of three. They are introduced by Claire and each read a poem, after which the audience responds vibrantly, their applause measured on the trusty clapometer. Every participating poet receives a much coveted Bristol Poetry Slam pen, and the most appreciated poets proceed to the semi-final.

The Break

In the break the hum from the audience is palpable, as they discuss the outcome of the heats. This is the time when the excitement of Slam infects the people; everyone has an opinion, everyone has their favourites, everyone realises that it is their enthusiasm that decides who rides and who slides...

2: The Semi-Final

Each poet performs one poem. The two top-scoring poets proceed to the final and automatically qualify for a place in the Bristol team at the next InterCity Championship.

3: The Final

A coin is tossed to determine who will go first and silence descends as the finalists take to the stage. Applause decides the outcome, and at the end of the evening The Winner is invited to perform an encore. There follows the award ceremony where the two finalists receive their certificates and prize money. DJ Steve Rice takes to the wheels of steel and the audience takes to the dance floor.

The Philosophy of Slam

The Bristol Poetry Slam believes that it is more important to stand up and allow your words to be heard, than it is to be a winner. We do our best to encourage a nurturing, supportive environment for embryonic performers to realise their potential before a large and enthusiastic audience. As Alan Wolfe, host of the Asheville, North Carolina Slam says: "The point is not the points; the point is the poetry."

* written by Bob Holman, organiser and host of The Nuyorican Poets Cafe Grand Slam, New York.

THE BRISTOL POETRY SLAM - Slam Records

DATE	VENUE	TYPE	1st	2nd	Guest
Tues. 13.12.94	Arnolfini, Bristol	Exhibition	Gerry King	Tim Gibbard	
Thurs. 9.02.95	Louisiana, Bristol	Open	Paul Coade	Sara-Jane Arbury	
Tues. 28.03.95	Brewhouse, Bristol	Open	John Kandinsky	Gillian Watt	Jem Rolls
Tues. 25.04.95	Brewhouse, Bristol	Open	Nick Moore	Rob Cookson	Marcus Moore
Tues. 30.05.95	Brewhouse, Bristol	Grand	Tim Gibbard	John Kandinsky	
Thurs. 15.06.95	Farrago, London	InterCity	Bristol	London	
Tues. 27.06.95	Flyer, Bristol	InterCity	Bristol	London	
Tues. 25.07.95	Flyer, Bristol	Open	J.Words	Roz Chissick	Spider Evans
Tues. 29.08.95	Flyer, Bristol	Open	Chris Colvin	Tony Lewis-Jones	Ruth McClaughny
Tues. 31.10.95	Flyer, Bristol	InterCity	Liverpool	Bristol	
Tues. 28.11.95	Flyer, Bristol	Grand	Tim Gibbard	John Kandinsky	
Tues. 30.01.96	Flyer, Bristol	Open	Ralph Hoyte	John Kelly	Tim Gibbard
Tues. 27.02.96	Flyer, Bristol	Open	Martyn Hudson	Polly Carr	Ifor Thomas
Tues. 26.03.96	Flyer, Bristol	InterCity	Cardiff	Bristol	
Fri. 26.04.96	Guildhall, Gloucester	Open	Avril Quantrill	J. Words	
Tues. 30.04.96	Flyer, Bristol	Open	Lucy English	Kevin McKeigue	
Tues. 28.05.96	Flyer, Bristol	Open	Ethos Sphere	Andrew Nash	Rob Gee
Tues. 25.06.96	Flyer, Bristol	InterCity	Bristol	Sheffield	
Tues. 27.08.96	Flyer, Bristol	Open	Marcus Moore	Claire Berry	Cynthia Hamilton
Tues. 24.09.96	Flyer, Bristol	Open	Peter Wyton	Gary Cox	
Wed. 25.09.96	St.Matthias College, Bristol	Exhibition	Tim Gibbard	J.Words	
Tues. 29.10.96	Flyer, Bristol	InterCity	Bristol	London	
Tues. 26.11.96	Flyer, Bristol	Celebration			
Tues. 28.01.97	Flyer, Bristol	Open	Gill Higgins	Nigel Pearce	
Tues. 25.02.97	Flyer, Bristol	Open	Tom Phillips	Mike Leeman	Georgia Varjas
Tues. 25.03.97	Flyer, Bristol	InterCity	Bristol	Brighton	
Wed. 02.04.97	Xcess Xpress, London	InterCity	Draw		
Tues. 29.04.97	Jesters, Bristol	Open	Toby Farrow	XMO555	Matthew Harvey
Wed. 07.05.97	Chapter, Cardiff	InterCity	Bristol	Cardiff	
Tues. 27.05.97	Jesters, Bristol	Open	Christine E Ramsey	Rosemary Dun	David Brown
Sun. 08.06.97	Volksfest, Bristol	Exhibition	J.Words	Tim Gibbard	
Tues. 24.06.97	Jesters, Bristol	InterCity	Manchester	Bristol	
Tues. 26.08.97	Jesters, Bristol	Open	John Trolan	Flo Kirk	Sophie
Tues. 30.09.97	Jesters, Bristol	Open	Emel	Rosemary Gamsa	Murray Lachlan Young
Tues. 28.10.97	Jesters, Bristol	InterCity	Bristol	Birmingham	
Tues. 04.11.97	Jesters, Bristol	UK Qualifier	J.Words/ Lucy English/	Ali/ Dot Matrix.	
Sun. 09.11.97	Jesters, Bristol	UK Qualifier	Tim Gibbard/ Tom Phillips/	Kevin McKeigue/ Gary Cox.	
Tues. 11.11.97	Jesters, Bristol	UK Qualifier	Ethos Sphere/ Emel/	Sheldon King/ John Trolan.	
Sun. 16.11.97	Jesters, Bristol	UK Grand Qualifier	Tim Gibbard/ Lucy English/	Emel/ Kevin McKeigue.	
Sat. 22.11.97	Watershed, Bristol	UK Champs.	Bristol	Edinburgh	Pink Sly

The Bristol Poetry Slam wishes to acknowledge the support and give thanks to the following:

Lesley Anne Rose, Mike George (Second Tuesday), Waterstone's, Venue magazine, Alison B (*strangefish*), Ralph (Bristol Flyer), Labbatts, Carlsberg Ice, Bristol City Council, Geni Hall (The Poetry Can), South West Arts, Marcus Moore (Cheltenham Festival of Literature), BBC Radio Bristol, Terry Downie (Bristol Education Centre), Dave, Paul and Jim (Jesters), The Baring Foundation, The Foundation for Sport and the Arts, The National Lottery through the Arts Council of England, GWR fm, Epics, Polly & Gill (Next Up), Nick (Grate Expectations), UK Poetry Slam Championship volunteers (Marjorie Carmichael, Philip Hudson, Florian, Spider Evans, Doug Nash, Joy Kahumbu, Anna Guest, Nick McCamphill, Mark Carter, Tony Guest, Jason Reed, Tony Lansdown, Marcus Colfer, Jason Davis, Stewart Wolf, Gill Higgins), Bablake Wines, Brymon Airways, Screen One, Hilton National, Eric Goornik (Magnetic Poetry), Greater Bristol Foundation, Blackwells, John Scott (Vale Publishing), Faber & Faber, Murray Lachlan Young, Pimp$ of the Alphab£t Press and all the poets and audiences who make The Bristol Poetry Slam possible.

Glenn Carmichael & Claire Williamson

IT'S SLAM TIME!

Lucy English
BRISTOL PEOPLE

Bristol People are happy people
they smile all the time
       because they're living in fluffy land
and they don't understand
there's a world out there
that doesn't care whether or not
they have Community Festivals and Poetry Slams

Bristol People are happy people
they smile all the time
because they're such good mates
and they can relate to almost anyone

So you can
crash round my house, you can sleep on my floor
you can sleep in my bed and what's more
you can sleep with me
and you're all my friends
so I'm going to be pretty busy

So come on down to Bristol town
and have some fun because we're all twenty-one

We've got   St. Vincent Rocks
We've got   Mud Dock
We've got   Cafe Latte
We've got   The Labour Party
We've got   a Comedy Club
We've got   a rub-a-dub hot tub
We've got   Poetry   hip-hip-hooray
We've got   a social mix
We've got   a quick fix
We've got   Council Tax
We've got   T.K. Maxx

We're so up front
so piss off you wimps

We've got cider pubs   and trendy bars
but we're so green   we don't like cars
We've got mountain bikes   our thighs are tight
When we play it right   we get fucked all night
We've got country walks   and talk talk talk

We've got a Centre for the Performing Arts
paid for by Lottery grants
We've got Cabot's boat
We've got a sea of dope
We've got urban decay and polluted air
and nothing's changed for a hundred years

We've got The Showcase   what a waste of space
We've got a ring road   overload
We've got streets of truth   and a council of lies
We've got big hair   we've got bright eyes
We're full of love   have you had enough?
And when you've had enough   you can get up the duff

And I quite forgot
somebody just got shot
in St. Paul's

Bristol People are happy people
they laugh all the time
        because they're living in fluffy land
and they don't understand
there's a world out there
that doesn't fucking care.

Tom Phillips

POETRY IS THE NEW ROCK 'N' ROLL

None of us really wants it, do we?
Poetry as the new rock'n'roll -
the fame, the fortune, the snowdrifts of cocaine?
The megastores stuffed with slim volumes,
the stadia packed with hysterical fans.
Seamus Heaney struts through his Greatest Hits
and Wembley goes mental for his retro 60's smash -
The Death Of A Naturalist.

At the Slam Awards, things get out of hand
when U.A. Fanthorpe does a Jarvis Cocker,
leaping on stage to punch out Ted Hughes.
Poetry Please puts MTV off air
and Chris Evans takes over *The South Bank Show*:
Thank Fuck It Isn't Melvyn Bragg.

Chased by balding journoes from *New Literary Express*
and Ivy League groupies begging them
to hold spontaneous writing workshops wherever they go,
a tourbus full of Britpoets breaks big in the States.
Attila the Stockbroker's guest appearance
on *Friends* is something else
and Benjamin Zephaniah dons his Elvis sequin jumpsuit
for a six month stint in Vegas.
Rumours that T.S. Eliot choked to death on his own vomit abound.

Tattoos of Auden and Sylvia Plath are openly worn
and *Now That's What I Call Metaphysical Poetry 57*
outsells the Oasis comeback album.
To save their failing careers,
The Spice Girls resort to hiring Pam Ayres.
Now that's what I want
what I really really want....

Everyone's looking for the elusive Bristol Sound
and Faber & Faber send A&R teams
to comedy clubs and the upstairs rooms of pubs
to sign unknown writers for six figure sums.

For Simon Armitage, though, it's all too much.
After winning the Battle of the Bards
and beating Wendy Cope to Number One,
he escapes to Iceland and releases a volume
of Lo-fi verse which marks a departure
from his popular mainstream work.
He becomes Huddersfield's Syd Barrett -
an acid-frazzled lesson to us all.
His last known poem is printed in *The Sun*.
He claims it is better to starve as a genuine artist
than to spend your life as a fat rich fucker
with houses in Hollywood, Chelsea and Cannes.
Everyone agrees that he must have gone mad.
Somewhere in an abandoned CD pressing plant,
a group of penniless popstars is dreaming of revenge.

Tim Gibbard

CYBERPUNK

I'm a space cadet, a head on legs,
A soul assassin living with society's dregs.
I've got an attitude,
The pop kid brood 'cause I'm loud and rude
And when I'm in the mood I talk computer,
I play commuter as I ready my hooter
For the pay day, the way day,
The, sniff, sniff, sniff, 14 gramme day.
Def Jam, Tequila slam,
Going to the cash point, seeing my man
For his speed, weed, Henbane seed.
Cracking my skull to the sound of Nosebleed
'Cause I'm coming on strong when I'm coming on drunk.
I'm the beer hunter, the Cyberpunk.
I'm a coke head but I ain't dead
'Cause I take what it takes to keep me out of bed.
Benzedrine, Atropine, Tartrazine, Morphine,
Getting on a high with my own Endorphins.
Crack, Smack, something black,
Bombers perhaps or a bottle of Jack.
Afghani, Manali, Lebanese, Nepalese,
Lambs Bread, Caramello, Acapulco, Double Zero,
Slatey, Soap Bar, Home Grown, Skunk,
I'm a Temple Ball burner, the Cyberpunk.
I'm a Hip Hop hippy and I shoot from the hip,
I've got a stiff upper lip 'cause I'm ready for the next trip.
Pucker up, pucker up, Ecstasy,
15 or 20 all for me
'Cause I buy in bulk and I make a saving
From the score, to the pub, to the club and I'm raving.
I've got rocks to roll, rhythm to booze,
From your undone DM's to your shiny shoes.

I've got Ragga, Reggae, Ska and Funk
'Cause I'm a Disco killer, the Cyberpunk.
I like it heavy, I like it hard,
I like it loud and I like the little cards
With the Supermen or the smiley faces.
Waving my hands to the lightning traces
'Cause it's LS, LS, LSD
Mushroom Magic, trips for free,
Psyloci, psyloci, ci, ci, ci, ci, cibin.
See the scene, it's fresh and it's thriving.
This is the life I feel more alive in,
Step up to the edge and I'll show you how to dive in.
From outer space to in your face,
I can take the pace of this human race
'Cause I'm on a mission, I'm living on junk,
I'm a wasteland warrior, the Cyberpunk.
I'm built to last, my body can take it,
I'm all for real, I don't have to fake it,
I set the record straight and then I break it
And if you wanna party well I'm the one to make it sweet.
I get them on their feet,
I give 'em a treat as I hit 'em with a new beat.
Tearing it up, I'm breaking it down,
I'll be kicking it in, in this and any other town.
Chewing it out Yo! Chunk by chunk
'Cause I'm MC Android, the Cyberpunk.

Martyn Hudson

JOURNEY IN POETRY

Transcendental mental lentil
Scribbles with a pencil
Inky swirls
Trough other worlds
One man
High octane
Radioactive
Adrenaline energy
Full speed
Head on
Full stop
Poet on a mission
Pieces in position
Itch called inspiration
Writing from the gut
Gutter roots;
Radiant growth
Mixed in mind's matrix
Art in the Rant
Spitting Sparks
Sharp Shards
Barbs for the Bard
Lines harder and heavier
Than any snow
Illicit and Explicit
Vague vagary
Swirling fantasy
Mystique mistiness
Coquettish frolics
Throbbing hydraulics
Pulsing; pounding; points
Basking in the task

Jekyll and Hyde
Whirlwind ride
Pictures of clarity
Symbolic second skin
Throwing syllables
To the wind
Searching for the note
Without end
The eternal chord
Pitch of perfection
Pinnacle of direction
The rhyme that reels
Tight as virginity
Feast with the Beast
Fly with the flow
Partake of the rhyme
Savour its essence
Like smooth smoke
Or fine wine
Thirst for first
A farce like fast
Solid lock binds
Honey suckle confines
Passing trance
Seize the chance
To capture and enhance
Residual emotion
Receding vision
With accurate precision
Skill at play
To orally display
Poetry a loaded weapon
Sharp as a blade
Poetry the bitch
Poetry the babe
Poetry the gift

Poetry the slave
Mentor and tormentor
Signature engraved
Poetry the key
Along knife edge quay
Setting third eyes free
Poetry a collage
Of hand picked words
Both meaningful and absurd
A ruse to delude
Perplex and confuse
A Muse to amuse
A means to an end
Agendas to amend
Wrongs set write
From rags to glad rags
Rich in experience
In peacock finery
Performance Poetry
Creative Anarchy
Slam DIVAS
DEVOS
And DEMONS
Praise the enigma
Of our exquisite art

Claire Williamson

THE QUEEN OF ARTS

Franz Kafka once wrote:
"How can anyone hope to hold someone with words alone,
when holding is what hands are for?"

- yet poets can make
hands out of words, delicate fingers from
careful configurations,
alliterations,
conversations between
vowels and consonants. Poets constantly perform
the impossible - they touch you in their absence:
Make your throat lumpy;
Make your heart thumpy;
They can give you the gift of love in
letters.

I have been led up the garden path by poets;
I have been laid by the hearth with poets;
Spent time in the bath with poets;
I've had a good laugh with poets;
I've been exploded apart by complete strangers:
exploring me,
gnawing me,
imploring me to
read,
perceive,
conceive

another dimension...

Poets paint pictures,
poets make music,
poets write plays - plays on words.

Have you heard? - poets are magicians, they can
capture life onto paper,
paper life onto walls,
they can walk across pages,
ages,
stages. Poets live forever!
Poets give up? - never!
Never give up.
Keep on writing.
Keep on exciting hearts and minds and
keep on fighting to free

The Queen of Arts -

Poetry.

Polly Carr

SLAM VIRGIN

I'm a slam virgin and
that applause was great foreplay, by the way...
And I need it cos
I'm shaking, quaking, almost crying
Is this fear, or desire?
I'm the trembling slam virgin
I feel the blood rush, the body blush
It's not just my scarf and hair that clash
I'm the terrified slam virgin, I've never done this before
and really I want to run for my life
but for me there's no fate worse than defeat
and I don't want to be pinned to my seat through fear
and be unable to share this slam feeling, it's a two way thing
but I'm a shaking slam virgin and really scared
What if I freeze and dry or choke and die here
on stage, in public?
With you I can't fake it
My heart's beating hard in my throat, at your feet
and I'm losing it, big time
but, yes, I want to
yes
I want you
irrational passionate unconditional
falling for
all of you and I don't even know you
well not all of you
and not all of you well
Does this make me the slam tart?
Nah, I'm all heart
I'm not precocious
but take no precautions
This is unprotected

and my word of warning
slamming is catching contagious infectious
I know it's true
If I remember it right I caught it from some of you in the first place
and I just want to
pass it on, get it on, so I can't back out now
wouldn't want to anyhow
You slammers gave me love amazed me with words fresh
fast and furious
laid back, laid out like treasures before me and this inspired me
and through writing I have learnt to let
my heart think, my mind feel, touch a new edge
and my feet have a will of their own and
find the deep end, my favourite space
and I don't want to stay safe intact out of trouble
so I'll burst the bubble
because
I love you
all of you
an emotion beyond my control
there's no possession in my soul
but
I'm still shaking from
making this first move
trying to be brave
behave
in a manner appropriate to
a shy slam virgin
but it's exciting
and I'm an adult and I'm consenting
unrelenting
I want to pause I want to stop but you have got me in your grip
I'm grasping gasping and I've lost my bottle
I think a small drink would be a good idea
loosen my inhibitions
lose my hesitance

not my innocence
but now I know despite my fear
it's good fun doing this with you up here
My trembling's increasing
what's the reason?
I think I'm feeling like I'm coming
down with something
This is fervour and it hurts
an ache from a need to spread the word
with so much love to share to spare to feel it go both ways
I need to give and live risky
I can only do my best and lose it
and really don't mind if I don't come first.
And some of you are virgins still
so if this night touches you come out
come up, be scared, feel the thrill, try a taste of this magic
cos it's seductive, addictive
not selective
and we'll still love you in the morning.
Virgin no more I'm not really a poet
just a word-slut an ink-scrubber
no grammar-lover
I'm cutting lines, breaking out of syntax and sentences
allowing the occasional rhyme to creep in
for the sake of it
so I can say for the record
I might trip up on hip hop and be a crap rapper but
a small part of me wants to be a slam slapper.

Marcus Moore

MAKING LOVE AND WRITING POETRY HAVE A NUMBER OF THINGS IN COMMON

1: take a clean sheet
2: leave a stain

Jean Hathaway
FORGIVE ME

Forgive me
I'm not wearing my Laura Ashley dress.

Forgive me
I've not brought my poems
fanned
in the perfect hand of magazines
you know, AMBIT, OUTPOSTS, PROSPICE...

Forgive me
they are not even sheathed in plastic folders
the ones I say you should use
they keep the pages quiet
don't interfere with the microphone.

Forgive me
there are no dove-tails to the poems
saying
"this one will tell you I was in love in '73
and walking a lesser-known ridgeway between......"
Who cares anyway?

Forgive me
I'm not sure I made time to brush my hair.

Forgive me
I'm shit scared
and the poems
on their plain pages
are vibrating.

Maggie O'Brien

UNWRAPPING POETRY

There's a craze,
a mal-aise
in the poetry scene.
Know what I mean?
Like Rupert Bear's on amphetamines.
What is it? It's 'Rap', it's crap,
it's slap-hap,
fast-timing,
easy rhyming,
so-called poetry
clap-trap!
It's pop-arting, ain't it ever?
Arty-farting and they never
STOP
the 'sling words together,
aren't I clever?'
LOT.
There's no skill, no refrain,
nothing given, nothing gained.
Impress the crowd,
shout loud.
Feeling, meaning, wit and depth
lost to volume, waste of breath.
Anyone with half a mind
can demonstrate this cheap kind
of fast, slick, bounding along,
crass, thick, sounding wrong
duff
stuff.
Listen up!

23

I really ain't that clever
just because I've
got -
a collection and selection,
predilection for inflection
with no mind to finer reflection
lot - of words in my head
jumbled and fumbled
which I'll spill out on you.
Give me some craft man
show me some graft and
some respect for long tradition
not dumb, random, loud transmission
of easy rhyming,
sleazy timing.
Better we be impressed
by content not chatter
not this raving clatter -
Ain't it time that this matter
were
addressed?

Keith Davey

A WORD IN YOUR ERA!

Glancing back through The Times an article caught my eye;
"A group of assailants has been charged with mugging the English
Language. A Court Reporter said the muggings were so prolonged that
the English Language may never be the same again!" The Judge said
"while he felt some empathy towards the Language the sentence would
be deferred!"

Well that explains it then. And all the time I thought it was me!
You see, in my day, I thought that -

Grass was for mowing.
Coke was put in the boiler.
Pot was something you cooked in.
Speed, well speed was my first Lambretta 200
And Acid, well acid was found in dark brown bottles
living 'high' on laboratory shelves.

A PC was the man in shiny boots with his clichéd "evening all."
Hardware was a bag of nails.
Software was a pair of fleecy-lined slippers.
Fax were what you learned at school.
A Hard Drive was a trip in pouring rain on the back of my scooter.
And Chips, well chips of course came swathed in newspaper with liberal
splashings of vinegar.

A Chinese Take-Away I called an abacus.
Poll Tax were small clips used by telephone engineers.
Satellite TV was what pyromaniacs did in an electrical store.
Channel 4 was a question not description as in "what's that channel for?"
CD meant shabby, unkempt or sordid.
ECU was a line of posh people.
Hotline was the result of gleaming embers on the sidings after the steam train
had passed by.

A Contraflow was the way the last drop of toothpaste disappeared up the tube.
GTI were the letters my best friend Jimmy scratched on the blackboard
"our teecher is a gti!"
Yes, you've guessed it.
In my day dyslexia wasn't recognised either!

Grant meant bestow, allow as a gift, not a short term loan.
UB was money paid to students all summer long.
UWE was but a gleam in a Principal's eye.
Mates were friends you didn't want around at every conceivable opportunity.
A Health Trust was a padded belt worn by people with trouble 'down there'.
Oral Sex meant talking to her first to check when her parents were returning.
Time Share meant being together and not a villa in Spain.
You got married and then you lived together.
Even nostalgia isn't what it used to be.......

So please forgive my dated prose and double entendres
As my literary field is full of creaking styles.
I've passed the second comma in my life sentence
But hope for a lot more words before I come full stop!!

Tom Phillips
SIGNIFICANCE

Seeing as we cannot be
the Beats who shout *Go! Go!*
and *All Right!* on that
Charlie Parker session
you bought cheap on CD
(you couldn't decide if the tracks
were lost works of genius
or out-takes of a fool),
let's drive into Gloucestershire,
up into the Cotswolds,
and gaze at trout
escaping the trout farm.

Seeing as we missed
Hemingway boxing with Pound
(Fitzgerald, Dos Passos and Joyce
were doubtless cheering them on)
and most of the politics
and all of the art
of the Twentieth Century
because we were born after the War,
let's drive into Gloucestershire,
up into the Cotswolds,
and gaze at trout
escaping the trout farm.

Seeing as we are not
Missing In Action in 'Nam
and we didn't get blitzed
on hash and jungle demons
so far out, man, we began
to believe we could never go home
to the careful suburban nightmare,

let's drive into Gloucestershire,
up into the Cotswolds,
and gaze at trout
escaping the trout farm.

Seeing as discussing
image music text with Barthes
and sexuality with Foucault
is out of the question
and we wouldn't understand
their sad *jouissance*
while they deconstructed
eight packets of Gitanes
and a gallon of coffee,
let's throw out all these books
and drive into Gloucestershire,
up into the Cotswolds,
and gaze at insignificant fish -
because that is the easiest way
for us to pass the time.

Peter Wyton

GROUNDHOG DAY ON ACACIA AVENUE

Acacia Avenue. Sunday morning.
Small child on tiptoe at crossing button.
Street empty of traffic. Cat licks itself.
Green man. Red light. Child changes pavements. Turns.
Cat licks itself. Street empty of traffic.
Small child on tiptoe at crossing button.
Sunday morning. Acacia Avenue.

> Acacia Avenue. Sunday morning.
> Small child on tiptoe at crossing button.
> Street empty of traffic. Cat licks itself.
> Green man. Red light. Child changes pavements. Turns.
> Cat licks itself. Street empty of traffic.
> Small child on tiptoe at crossing button.
> Sunday morning. Acacia Avenue.

Acacia Avenue. Sunday morning.
Small child on tiptoe at crossing button.
Street empty of traffic. Cat licks itself.
Green man. Red light. Child changes pavements. Turns.
Cat licks itself. Street empty of traffic.
Small child on tiptoe at crossing button.
Sunday morning. Acacia Avenue.

> Acacia Avenue. Sunday morning.
> Small child on tiptoe at crossing button.
> Street empty of traffic. Cat licks itself.
> Green man. Red light. Child changes pavements. Turns.
> Cat licks itself. Street empty of traffic.
> Small child on tiptoe at crossing button.
> Sunday morning. Acacia Avenue.

GROUNDHOG DAY ON ACACIA AVENUE

Christine E. Ramsey

This is a poem of the lives that made no history.
of the people who lived and loved and died
and made no history.
of the child's laughter
of the woman's laughter
of the man's laughter
that is not always heard
and never
makes history.

Steven Prescott

THE BIGGER PICTURE

Unless one of my
brothers was involved
the news didn't really
bother us much,
though I do remember
the Pope getting shot
(us being catholic and all)
and when Chernobyl went up
we were watching the telly
while having our tea
and even the old man stopped eating,
scratched his belly and said
"sheesh" before asking
for the salt. World events
don't get much bigger
than that.

Adam Horovitz

THE LLOYDS PRAYER

Our manager, who art in mammon,
      bankrolled be thy name.
Thy pay-cheques come,
        thy mortgages be done,
in Lloyds, as it is in Midland.

Give us this day our daily interest
        and forgive us our late payments,
as we forgive those who make late payments unto us.
        Lead us not into the red
and deliver us from bailiffs,
                        for thine is the Government,
                        the politician and the Tory
                        on the never-never

            AMEN

Rob Cookson

PARTY PRICKS

Fuck off Major, Lib-Dems, New Labour
for I daydream of change and it's truth I'll wager
I'm sick of your false smiles and endless solutions
and hope for better times, real people, revolutions

Don't tell me again for I don't wish to hear
how much I can spend on health care or beer
I live in fear
of your changes for mistakes have been many
and the price has been high for those without any homes
holidays   helipads   hairdressers
chesterfields   cleaners   golf clubs   suit presses

I'm weary of you all and this sentence I shout
YOU CONDITION A LIFE YOU KNOW NOTHING ABOUT
for most of you were brought up sheltered and warm
and upon leaving Uni there was protection reborn
in the shape of parties, clubs, clans and clicks
a circle of people that you're safe to mix
can you hear me
do you hear me
you pricks

Maggie O'Brien

BULLOCKS

Britain's in crisis and the whole world's heard
all cos some mad cow's been spreading the word
that our food's impregnated with insanity seeds
maddeningly threatening humanity's greed.
A couple of mad cows and they suddenly relate
to the fact we've got insanity piled up on our plates.
Well I don't know about you but I find it quite funny
that sanity gets on the agenda when it's costing big money.
Not funny 'ha ha' but funny 'peculiar' it seems
I mean don't you wanna know who's defining what 'sanity' means?
When knock on most people's minds normally and no-one's at home
they're busy frying their brain cells with the cellular phone
while kids' limbs are blown off with the left-overs of mines
and wealthy religions still suck on poor minds.
We've got warring Arabs taking a tea-break to pray
and a third of the world doesn't eat anyway.
We've got semtex, chemicals, missiles, tanks,
the world's forests reduced to DIY planks,
a hole in the ozone and genetic selection,
some jerks killing rhino to get an 'erection' ?
World politicians lying through their teeth
'Yeah right! The greatest threat to my sanity's beef!'
Why on earth should burgers be the worst of my fears
when the sane have called me a mad cow for years?
We've got corruption, genocide, pollution and rage
and what do we come up with? A pink fluffy New Age
where we smoke Sunday joints saying "Chill out, where's the harm huh?"
and that we need to balance our chakras and accept it as karma!
What? Accept that 90% of all riches
is in the hands and pockets of some real sons of bitches
like the cocaine barons who could, don't forget,
personally wipe out the US national debt,
that the Queen of England's worth 10 million pounds
with exploitation and poverty still doing the rounds,

thousands living in the new cardboard cities
while Governments? They masticate on the real nitty-gritty
like what manure they can sling in the coming campaign
and how they all get elected again,
and all of this stuff that eats away at the brain
isn't threatening to drive them insane?
I think someone should tell them to relax you know.
They all went stark raving bonkers a long time ago.
What, the contaminated food chain or oceans of crap
isn't driving them doolally tap?
I am getting madder but not from eating beef for God's sake
where else would my sanity be but at stake?
This is one mad cow who's not buying any of it
and I call for an embargo on global bullshit!

Ralph Hoyte

ME-TING

Went to see The Man the other day but him was 'inna me-ting'.
Dem **always** 'inna me-ting'
- dem sit there like sheep, all bleating!
When dem gone lunch dem 'inna me-ting'
Dem a stuff dem face an' call it eating!
When dem gone home early dem 'inna me-ting'
An' I-man trying to survive an' tekkin a beating!
When dem gone toilet dem 'inna me-ting'
Is about de only time dem a do a real ting!
Dem was **born** 'inna me-ting'!
Dem will **dead** 'inna me-ting'!
"Hey, Miss, I been waiting 2 hour and him no show. Is a wha'g'wan,
hey?"
Ms Frost-an-Ice she curl her lip an' say, "Sorry, sir, him inna me-ting."
Is a who dem tink dem a treating -
so?
Come mek me give dem a fleeting -
blow!
Eh!
Me jus' realise is why dem a call it a **me**-ting
- is 'cos is a ting for "**ME, ME, ME**"
dem don' concern themself with nobody else.

So me done call the whole world to a **WE-TING**
then **dat** is a ting for everybody!

Danny McCue

THE MILLENNIUM

THE WINDOW MISTED, CONDENSATION, DAMP
ANOTHER COLD NIGHT ON THE STREETS FOR THE 20TH CENTURY TRAMP
ANOTHER RESTLESS NIGHT UNDER THE 20TH CENTURY STARS
AS THE 20TH CENTURY PRISONER WAITS
BEHIND SELF-MADE 20TH CENTURY BARS.

THESE YEARS BEFORE THE MILLENNIUM, HAS ANYTHING REALLY CHANGED?
PEOPLE STILL DIE BECAUSE THEY CAN'T AFFORD TO BE SICK
SPIRITUAL POVERTY IS STILL THE SAME.

CYCLES WITHIN CYCLES, MONTHS GROW INTO YEARS
INVENTIONS PROFOUND AT THE SPEED OF SOUND
MAN'S HEART STILL FULL OF FEAR
ONE HUNDRED YEARS COME AND GONE, INDUSTRIAL & TECHNOLOGICAL AGE
ONE HUNDRED BILLION TEARDROPS IN AN OCEAN OF SADNESS AND RAGE.

HUNGER THE BIGGEST KILLER
BEING POOR THE BIGGEST CRIME
I WONDER HOW THIS CENTURY WILL BE RECORDED
AS IT IS WRITTEN IN THE BOOK OF TIME
NEATLY AND COMPLETELY OR OF HOW IT RANGES INDISCREETLY
FROM THE RIDICULOUS TO THE SUBLIME.

NOT ALL THIS CENTURY IS MELANCHOLY
NOT EVERYTHING TURNED OUT BAD
MYSELF, I'VE A SENSE OF FREEDOM
A REALITY FAR LESS SAD.

IT'S EASY TO LOOK ON THE NEGATIVE
FAR HARDER TO LOOK FOR THE GOOD
WHAT THE WORLD NEEDS NOW IS COMPASSION
THE SEED OF SPIRITUAL FOOD.

THE STRONGEST ROOTS AND THE HEALTHIEST FLOWERS
ARE DETERMINED BY THE AMOUNT OF DECAY
THAT BEING THE CASE HOPE IS BORN
IN THE SOIL OF YESTERDAY.

BANGY (Prayer E.B.)

My spotlight fades,
I feel you wait,
your fingers round the trigger grip,
now you run scared, your fingers slip.

Message from a poet,
"No sanctuary for a murderer."

You know I tried to end your war,
you know I tried to cure your ill,
you know I tried to change your world,
in ecstasy you speed your thrill.

Now with your hands infront your eyes
you shut love out, keep hurt inside.
Now with your hands infront your eyes
your destiny has made you blind.
Now with your hands infront your eyes
true unity is hard to find.

(When I close my eyes I can only see the
vision of Bangy being blown away,
no matter how much pain I feel in life I only
want to understand the reasons why Bangy
was blown away that night,
can you tell me the reasons why Bangy was blown
away that night?)

Bangy, with your words you came you found me,
you tried to make me understand,
show me a safe reality,
take the weapons out of my hands.

Bangy, life told us love would find a way,
    now you tell me that I'm alone,
    now do you hear all what I say?
    do you feel how my fears have grown?

    Now my heart by hurt is haunted,
    now that I feel you are not close,
    now my thoughts of you distorted,
    you are the one I need the most.

    Born from 'A' fire our bright light shone eternity,
    a strange desire I look upon now that I know
    you set me free,

    "I speak my mind."

Julie Boston

JUSTICE FOR MARLON THOMAS CAMPAIGN

What made Marlon Thomas drop out of hi-tec, hard-sell Brunel?

Was it the gloom of the lecture room?
Or the regimentation and isolation?

Was he ignored? Or bored?
Did he eat where profits are stored?

Was it the student union section
where pool and confectionery make the connection
and empower those in command
to stifle united demand?

What made Marlon Thomas drop out
of this fun-crusher, hope-shredder, soul-starver
agent of narrow profit margins
is what makes me want to
investigate the fairground attack
by a vigilante pack
on anyone black.

Angus Brown

PURPOSEFUL DIALOGUE

WHEN YOU ENTER INTO DIALOGUE WITH ME
PLEASE MAKE SURE IT'S SENSE YOU TALK
FOR I'VE NO TIME
FOR SIDE-SHOWS OR COMEDY ACTS
OR TO LISTEN TO GUILT
OR OBTUSE CHATTER.
WHAT MATTERS
IS FLOW OF THOUGHT
AND CONSTRUCTIVE DEBATE -
BY CREATING COMMON GROUND
WE RID OURSELVES OF IGNORANCE
ARROGANCE AND PREJUDICE
WE SPEAK THE SAME LANGUAGE.

IT IS THROUGH THE MEDIUM OF WORDS
THAT WE ARE ABLE
TO SWAP IDEAS AND BELIEFS
ATTEMPTING TO UNDERSTAND EACH OTHER
BY APPRECIATING AND ACKNOWLEDGING
OUR DIFFERENT PERCEPTIONS
AND EXPERIENCES OF THE WORLD.
IT IS THROUGH THIS MEDIUM
THAT WE ARE ABLE
TO TRULY EXPRESS OURSELVES
SHOWING OUR FEELINGS
DISPLAYING OUR INTEGRITY
ABSORBING EACH OTHER'S BACKGROUND
OUR ROOTS AND CULTURE.
PLEASE FORGIVE ME
WHEN I SAY TO YOU:
WHEN ENTERING INTO DIALOGUE WITH ME
DON'T BE ABRASIVE, ABUSIVE OR BASHFUL

BE YOURSELF.
DON'T BE FRIGHTENED
TO FEEL YOUR OWN HEART
AS YOU SPEAK -
WE'RE BOTH ON COMMON GROUND
YOU AND I
SO, FOR THE SAKE OF HUMANITY
LET'S TALK SENSE.

Kathie Vallin

SPEAK OUT

There is a poet which lies within us all.

Get up, speak out
and let it be heard.
Don't hold back,
don't be afraid,
it's never too late
to tell your tale.
Let your words form
and go with the flow,
for you can never tell
which path it might take.
Meandering here,
ambling there,
dashing off on tangents
everywhere.
No matter if it hasn't an end,
capture the start
and take it from there.
Poems don't need
hard and fast rules.
Take it from me,
it's easy to do.

Just let go and let your poems free.

NO

NO   NO   NO
My favourite word.
The most delicious, exciting and reactionary word.
N. O. NO.
Nnn-o-o-o, what a word.
It's short, it's sweet,
It says it all and it's so powerful
NO... NO... NO...
What a word for a woman to use, no?
Men never believe it when they hear us use it.
Do you think I'm handsome?   No.
Wanna go out with me?   No.
Wanna go to bed with me?   No.
What, eh? Come again, they say.
You're talking to me me me!
No, oh no, no, no, no, oh no no no.
What weight it carries, such meaning, no?
And how easy it is to pronounce.
Nnnn-o-o-o-o-o.
A tiny little word you can put in your pocket
And just keep pulling out all day with the
Most dynamic effect.
And what an erotic word it is as well.
Nnooo   Nnoooo   Nnnooooo   Ohh Nnoooooo
OH NO, you came!
Then there is the silent No.
You can nod it.
You can shake it.
You can wag it.
It always means No.
You can dress it up with fancy clothes like
Nah, Nixt or Nope

You can emphasise it like No never, No nothing, No way, No chance.
But in its pure naked state, that two-lettered word,
Oh that two-lettered word.
And what if Princess Di had said "No" to Charles?
And what if Mrs. Thatcher's mum had said "No" to her husband?
And what if Marilyn Monroe had said "No" to Bob and John?
And what if Desdemona had said "No" to Othello?
And what if one day all we Women said "No"?
What a magic little word.
My favourite, deliciously simple two-lettered word.
NO.

Tony Lewis-Jones

ROMAN HOLIDAY

In Rome, the only summer
we holidayed together,
at a table on the pavement
staring at the Pantheon,
you said that you were

sick of paintings
sick of me
and sick of bloody Italy.
We took a taxi back to the hotel
and I thanked St. Peter you were paying.

You spent the rest of the week
buried in our room.
When at last we stepped on to the train
you managed to smile
and, offering an end to our vendetta
told me I'd write about this one day.

I remember saying
there are some things
you don't write about.

Ray Gange

ROMEO IS BLEEDING

romeo is bleeding
once more
his entrails
strewn across the city
he refuses all help
and waits
vainly
for juliet
to come and
tend his wounds
the paramedics
want to
feed him morphine
to ease his
suffering
but he will not
let them
for though
the pain is
killing him
at least
it reminds him
of her

Paul Coade

WHAT IS THE POINT?

Do you really wanna know
What I wish?
OK then
If you're ready
I'll tell you what I wish
I wish
I wish you wouldn't just sit there and snigger
And figure you can work it all out
I wish you would relax
Take it easy
Why don't you ask me?
I'll tell you what it's all about
It's about
                    Look
It is about time you knew
So stop what you're doing and listen to me
I promise not to take more than a moment
Or two
Put your feet up
Unwind
Then take a deep breath
Conserve your energy
If you've got any left
                    I'm
Finding this hard
So before I go on
I will admit that it may be just me
I could be seeing things that are simply not there to see
I'm probably going too far with this curiosity
But please listen
Please be open-minded
I know you're capable

But thought you may need reminding
                              It's as if
It's like
Oh OK alright
I'll be more direct
It's got to the stage where it's becoming a chore
Trying to get through to you
And give you that which I just haven't got any more

                                                        No

No it's not your fault and neither is it mine
We've both drifted
Become fragmented and tormenting
About to cross the thin line

Yes I do know how it started
I can tell you exactly when
But when I do
Please don't cry
I'll take responsibility for my part
And I really will try to put myself in your shoes
Yes you do deserve some credit
And yes you have paid your dues
But living together
                              Well
It's becoming bad news

Why are you pointing?
Don't point
Don't point
I'll come to my point
The point is
The point is I can't see the point in us
Continuing to pretend
That everything is rosy and cosy
When it's obviously the end
                              What

What
What do you mean you agree?
And why are you looking like that at me?
Look I don't think you quite grasp
Or understand what it is that I'm saying
I'm saying it's over sweetheart
And I'm tired of delaying and postponing
My time just for you
I wanna be one
I'm sick and tired of being half of two
Especially when the other half is you
Don't sit there and nod with that smug smile on your face
Aren't you concerned that I'm out of this place?

                                        Glad?

Glad!
You can't be glad   I thought
I thought   we had something good
Something at least worth fighting for
I thought you would stop me
                     Beg me
Not to walk out of the door
What is it?
What's wrong?
Don't you love me any more?

Of course you do
Forgive me I'll stay it was only a bad joke
You know I don't really want to end it
Blow it all up in smoke
                     Pardon?
What do you mean it's too late?
That you've found someone else?
You're so spiteful and selfish
I don't believe it
              I can't take it

How could you when I've treated you so good?
After all we've been through?
I never thought you would do this to me
Come on
                              Tell me the truth
Has he been here and slept under my roof?
I'm sorry I didn't mean to say mine
I meant to say ours
                              Oh now I get it
That's where those smelly flowers came from
OK   OK
You have it your way
But I'm keeping the flat
And everything in it
And anything that reminds me of you
I'll   bin it or sell it!
Alright I've heard enough
                              Get out
                              Shut the door
And don't bother writing
                    Or phoning
      I don't want to see you
                              Any more!

                    Sssshhhit

Sara-Jane Arbury
LIVING TOGETHER

Waking
Shaking
Walking
To the bathroom
Defecating
Urinating
Washing
Brushing
Flushing
The toilet

Is This It?

Shopping
For food
Cooking
The food
Eating
The food
Excreting
The food
OH!
It's such Fun!
It's just Great!
It's Fantastic!

Is This It?

Watching TV
Making cups of tea
Watching TV
Making cups of coffee

Watching TV
Richard and Judy
Watching TV
Anne and Nick

Is This It?

Brookside
Neighbours
Eastenders
Young Doctors
Home and Away
With you each day

Is This It?

Shake and Vac
Mr. Muscle
Flash Excel
Daz or Persil
Danny Baker
Our whites are whiter
Cos Living Together
We help each other
Choose the right powder
From
Spar
Asda
Kwik Save
Lo-Cost
Co-Op
Tesco's
Aldi
(Where beans are 7p)
Sainsbury's
Safeway
Gateway

WOH!!!
Every day's a holiday!
A win on the lottery!
Cute and cuddly!

Is This It?

Room to move
We have
Room to move
We move
From the bedroom
Move
To the living room
And
Hoover
Polish
Dust
Wipe
Cleanse
Purify
Sterilize
Fumigate
Sanitate
Decontaminate
Our Very Own Love Nest
It's The Best!
Bugger The Rest!

Is This It?

We have no chicks
We are careful
Reliable
Responsible
We take it in turns
To take precautions

Condom
Femidom
Condom
Pill
Condom
Diaphragm
Condom
Coil
Condom
Injection
Condom
Sponge
OH WE ARE ONE!!!

He buys me Immac
Lil-lets and Tampax
I buy him Mycil
Gillettes and Ex-Lax
Oh and
Condoms
Condoms
Loads 'n' loads
Of 'em
And we go to bed
Clean and shiny...

And dread
Waking up
To another
New day
Cos
We both know it
But
We won't show it
That
We hate the fact
That

This

Is

It.

Andrew Nash

THE BATH THAT KEEPS OUR PAST ALIVE

As disgusting as it may seem
my bath still holds the water
in which we bathed all those years ago.
I will admit that it has left a thick film on it
and the dead skin left on the rim of the bath
could almost be alive again,
small animals have even found a home there
but it is a part of the house now
I just cannot pull the plug.
And somehow, after all these waveless nights,
the roses are still living and bobbing
like lifebuoys on the grimy surface
as if markers of our sex.
Every nowandthen
in those mindless moments we all have
when we slink off into our pasts
and allow ourselves to go frivolously free,
I bathe in the scum of our lives
and when the cold soaks through my clothes
I play with the chain that could suck it all away
but I just cannot pull the plug.

John Trolan

BELIEVE IN LOVE

First impressions,
Pure intentions,
Chasing a love
That lasts forever,
Augurs well for nights of passion,
Believe in love, believe me.

Wet sex sessions
Are thirsty ardours,
Tongues embrace
To replenish each other.
I could drink like this forever,
Believe in love, believe me.

Unspoken confessions
Precede the inevitable:
Passion will perish,
Appetite go absent.
Kiss bewilderment, let it happen
And believe in love, believe me.

Wretched expressions
Reveal the effort
Required to deny
Burnout has happened.
Someone said "Nothing lasts forever"
Still, believe in love. Believe.

Mary Petrie

THIS THING CALLED LOVE

Love is a strange thing.
No-one has really defined it,
but when you're in love, you know.

Love is a strange thing.
It can be hard to love those we don't like,
but they still need our care.

Love is a strange thing.
The pleasure and the pain can become so close,
they're almost the same emotion.

Love is a strange thing.
Jesus said "The greatest love a man can have for his friends
is to give his life for them."
And then, just to prove he knew what he was talking about,
he went out and did just that.

Love is a strange thing.

Mike Leeman

IN THE DEEP MID-MORNING

In the strange half-land
Between
Sleep
And
Awake
I stare at you
Whilst you lie there
Sleeping
Unconscious
Considering
Complications
And all sorts
I lie there
And stare
At your unmoving
Form
Forming thoughts
Of
Past
Future
Combined
Intertwined
Together
Forever.
You awaken slightly
And smile
Through dream drenched eyes
Then close to other dreams
I meanwhile
Awake dream my own dreams
And smile to myself
And to an unlooking
You.

Gerry King
WITHOUT LOVE

I embrace a girl outside Walthamstow dog track.
I've got that contentment that comes with a wrap.
She wants a baby, she always sterilises her vibrator in Milton.
It is a consumer's affair. The batteries come from the radio.
My stars are encouraging.
The fist of revolution is daubed on a wall.
The car I drive is a left hooker.
Will I feel different tomorrow?

Thoughts come quicker than a sympathy fuck after a four year stretch.
Where would you be without love?

Without love the Sistine Chapel would have been painted by numbers.
And cinemas all over the world would constantly show 'Metropolis'.
Lipstick would carry a warning "Kissing can lead to love."
Without love The National Gallery would be derelict.
And the Taj Mahal just another take-away.
Without love puppies would be born fully grown.
And couples banned from boating lakes.
Without love erogenous zones would be junctions off the M25.
And honeymoon suites foreign language laboratories.
Without love every tourniquet would have studs.
And rushes would be controlled by British Rail and constantly delayed.
Without love I'd be back with you.

Ethos Sphere

SHIN-DIG HEART

Words run down the wall.
Block out the cold, lock the door.
We're very different, just swim the same pool,
branded with a feeling you cannot ignore.
Trying to understand natural law,
given less when you wanted more.
Accepting circumstance, standing apart, J'adore.
Won't something come to break my fall?
Animal tear up the roots, rip the binding,
havoc blinding, chemical tiding.
Given the short straw.
Wiery, harshly, fiery, starry-eyed,
"What's this shit I've been supplied?"
Try to make it again on my own,
now in the past the flights I've flown,
now in the ground the seeds I've sown,
whittled to the bone.
Homegrown, roughed up, bitten, knackered, sceptic,
what I had I should have kept it.
Into another space I go.
I'm tired of chasing, waiting, missing, wanting, waiting...

You don't know what you've lost
until it's gone.

Errand Singlett

THE POINT OF NO RETURN

IT HAS NO BEGINNING AND NO END YET SOMEWHERE IN THE MIDDLE IS
THE POINT OF NO RETURN.
IT'S THE POINT THAT DETERMINES LIFE OR DEATH.
IT'S THE POINT THAT GIVES YOUR LEGS THAT JELLY FEELING.

IF SOMEONE ASKED YOU TO POINT TO THE POINT OF NO RETURN
THEY COULDN'T BECAUSE IT'S A PERSONAL THING.
HOWEVER, EVERY PERSON CAN PINPOINT IT TO THEMSELVES.

WHEN I SAY POINT I DON'T MEAN POINT AT ME OR POINT AT SOMEONE OR
EVEN A SHARP POINT, I MEAN THE POINT OF NO RETURN.

YOU CAN FIND IT TOO, GO OUT INTO YOUR BACK GARDEN, STAND UP
RIGHT ON TOP OF A WALL AND LEAN FORWARD EVER SO SLOWLY
UNTIL YOUR BRAIN SENDS A MESSAGE TO EVERY MUSCLE IN YOUR
BODY, PULL BACK, PULL BACK.

IF YOU DON'T PULL BACK YOU WILL HAVE GONE THROUGH THE POINT
OF NO RETURN.
THERE IS ONLY ONE SIGN THAT POINTS OUT THE POINT OF NO RETURN.
THAT SIGN IS A FACIAL EXPRESSION OF FRIGHT AND THRILL AND
I'M
GOING TO SHIT MYSELF.

Tôpher Mills

RUTH ON THE ROOF

RUTH!

RUTH!

What are you doing on the roof
RUTH?
Come down off the roof
RUTH!
Is that a bottle of Vermouth
RUTH?
You shouldn't be drinking Vermouth
on the roof
RUTH!
You might fall and break a tooth
RUTH!
Come down off the roof
RUTH!
Just because you've lost your youth
RUTH!
What do you mean I'm being uncouth
RUTH?
I'm not being uncouth
RUTH
It's the truth
RUTH!
No I can't give you proof
RUTH!
Come down off the roof
RUTH!
Stop being a goof
RUTH!

RUTH!

RUTH?

Where are you,
have you taken to the hoof
RUTH?
This is just a bit too aloof
RUTH!
You've gone from the roof
RUTH!
What have you done with the Vermouth
RUTH?
Is this some kind of spoof
RUTH?

RUTH!

RUTH! ! !

RUTH! ! ! ! !

OHHHHH
STREWTH !

Alexander Grant

ABOUT TO FALL

Relax.
Rest once more,
The guilt that scratched
Is now ignored.
Relax.
Spill a sigh,
No humbling need
To apologise
For anything.
Throwing
The dice,
Staking the sweetest guarantees,
A life,
The peace.
Giddy heights, the air is hard to breathe.
Everything's covered in us.
Everything's smothering us.
Loosen up,
Listen in,
This is no time for broken wings.

Marcus Moore

DAY IN THE LIFE OF

midnight. scream. i'm alive.

the small hours are snug secure
with parental bedside lamp

adolescence a seeping dawn
finding peers through the gloom

at 6am i get up, go to work
i can drink drive smoke vote fuck

mid-day: mid-life; no crisis
only older wiser bolder wider

but just where did the morning go?
working smoking fucking i suppose

the afternoon drifts towards tea-time
i glance at the clock, fashion it thus:

> in the day of my life
> if i get my three score
> ten and a couple more
> then the time at the third stroke of now
> is 3.24pm and 6 seconds precisely
>
> this time tomorrow
> another $3^1/2$ seconds
> will have elapsed
> and in a year from now
> i shall be nearly a quarter to four

i must finish what i'm writing
eat, change, go out, see some friends

i shall stay in the pub until long after closing time
just in case today's the day

the clock goes forward

Roger Day

CERTAIN

The rat walks the maze. It paces the cage,
fed once an hour by a hand from a crack
in the sky. It sniffs the walls once more.
It knows shine and shade, day from night.

The map is the truth: North, East, South, West.
The walls will be there next time I bump them,
and the night sky wheels on and on and on,
and the world is firm and full and fair as I go.

I go for a walk at dusk, a run at dawn.
Blood pumps, heart thuds. I try to stop.
Leaf turns from green to red to mulch;
a balm for the day the calm is there as Im

always treadling lethargic whitelines avoiding roaring
greasedspeed bending over corners
articulated monsters bludgeoning
butterfly hedgehog starling weasel wildness
confusional contusions looking over blankets
antiviral cleanliness harbouring listlessness
feeling something nothing looking prosthetics
extension scarlet kindness
                            becoming bleeding undoing
kidneys slowing exchanger
406 406 406 204 104 444 filters
into liquidity sinking into sewage systems
into geomantic liquid river formations
crusting lazily under constellatic fuzziness
dusty darkness
                    hurtling spinning spherical feeling

everything ocean spatial coordinates endless tipping
dripping solidity firmness
                          leading illusionwise
bearings multiply
                  plaster charts dereferencing nothing

cannot connect   cannot connect   cannot connect

Kate McCue
DESPERATELY SEEKING SOMETHING

They are storming the spiritual realm,
Pillaging each bliss station,
Collecting 'peak experiences'.
Rushing, pushing, stealing, snatching.
The intensity addicts,
Come to conquer the fearful enemies,
The fearful enemies of our groaning, aching humanity.

Crystals sparkle in every window across the land,
Bookshelves bulge and sag, screaming out a printed chaos of philosophies,
Candles drip coloured wax, congealing into solid lumps that float
Across the scented waters of every aromatherapeutic bath.

Advertisements in every expresso flowing café,
The ultimate workshop is today,
The meaning of life and why we are here,
Just £300 and all will be clear.

The lost and lonely gather in desperate groups,
Clinging to each other,
Careful to hold tight to the masks
That cover each face in fixed expressions of serenity.

And those with the dazed, glazed eyes,
Wrapped in the insane hallucinations of television,
Televisions put in place of a hearth in every home,
What can this mean?

All equally enslaved in continuous outpourings
Of fantasy and illusion.
Fill up that hole.
Stuff and hoard the dirty paper inside fat wallets
To buy an identity, a meaning, a life.

So much and so much more, until we are
Fat, sated, bloated, drunk, stoned and dazed
And we do not notice that we are all falling
Into the void.

And we will not notice,
Until we finally arrive
And realize
Just how homesick we are, bereft and scarred.

Whatever takes us through the void,
No one can avoid
Standing at the doorway
Which leads to our wholeness.

Lesley Anne Rose

WALKABOUT

They used to go "Walkabout"
When the spirit called their name,
A vast mysterious wilderness - without and within,
New territory - New heights - New depths.

Everyone someday hears the cry for "Walkabout"
Feels the need to explore alone,
A wild instinct awakes inside,
The passion for solitude overwhelms,
Journey alone - but never lonely,
Journey alone - yet always in company.

A life still full of friends and love,
Much to give and much to grasp,
Never taking for granted all that's offered,
Appreciating everything that's shared,
And caring more than most will ever know.

But dare to ask for what I crave?
I crave to go "Walkabout"

Christine E. Ramsey

here i am, moving still, lost
in a sea of street.   the hail
stones are huge today.   time slows.   most
people run by, i think; they sail
past, quickly.   meanwhile, i am
stuck.   these feet carry me home,
somehow (i choke) these goddamn
tears (on my throat) make unknown
(help) the rain (oh god) makes walls
to walk through but i can't i
can't believe (the world dissolves
above me, a cloud of why,
        and i can barely hear behind my wheezing)
        (grief is a hand on your heart that won't stop squeezing

J. Words

A HORRIBLE THOUGHT

Green Button please, Green Button!
I'm lying in bed, I can't feel my toes,
I can smell..... Hospitals.
I feel numb and kind of sick,
The Clock ticks.
I can hear...
"It's been 5 months now
And there has been no fluctuation
In the electrograph pattern."
Ah, that voice, deeper than the cut
Of any surgeon's knife.
It used to be husband and wife
But now it's Doctor and poor distraught
Woman discussing my life.
Apparently there's blood coming out of
The corner of my mouth now,
And I can't even muster a cough,
All I can think of is
Please! Don't switch me off.
If I'm nearly dead but still alive,
It's still my head, so I'll drive.
Because my life, when it comes to the
Crunch, is a, uh, uh, stay where you are,
Don't drive my car, lean, mean, my machine,
And it'll be my mistake if I miss the
Brakes,
And my crumpled mess, I guess.
But I keep the key in the ignition
Locked on, so for as long as the wheels
Turn, I can still go, so don't take me
For gone, give me a tow,
I'm still turned on, so please,
Don't switch me off!

When I'm dead, celebrate my life,
There'll be no point in crying.
But for as long as blood runs through
My head, I'll keep trying,
I'm not frightened of dying
And I'm not lying, now,
But when I am,
Please, don't switch me off.
It's a big choice to make,
So if I'm in no fit state
Then wait 'til I'm awake,
And it'll be my decision
Which I won't take
Because living's my mission,
So, please,
Don't switch me off!

Ione Stansfield

HIP

My mother in an open ward
is frail and translucent
as a leaf in sunlight.

Tubes burrough into her
lead out of her
take the blood away
spill the blood back in.

She is no longer whole.
A piece of metal
the size and shape of a boomerang
resides next to her pelvis
mutilates her.

But
she is learning to like
Coronation Street
Polos
Woman's Own
is getting good at
hurling things across the room,
shouting 'catch' to the other patients.

I feel helpless
so obey when she says
look for that grape I threw
it's somewhere under the other beds.

Zed Moore

NUMBERS AND LABELS

And there are millions of us in this queue
Called the Health Service.
The cold unwanted of perpetual motionless -
Waiting for the surgeon's stainless steel blade,
Looking for the mundane stethoscope,
And watching the brooding face of death
Looming over the smog.
We wait for our numbers, our labels
And horror and despair continually leap forth
To float majestically in to the void.
The poor, sooted faces of a hospital stare -
A vacant stare:
They have seen these numbers
And many more,
They have given these labels
And many more,
They have noted these failures
And many more.
But the walls are personified with the face of
Blood on Blood.
We are a statistic, a failing of society -
A slab of meat, A case study,
A few stitches, A knife,
A day's work, A new idea,
An obs chart, A nice clean saline drip,
An incision, An extension of their technology -
A Soundless voice in the hearts of Death.
As it snows and hails, we stand and wait -
Oh Patient Patients!
Pathetic poor wretches in need of whatever -
But no name, no brain, no heart, just pain,
In a never ending queue that is always the same.
But never quite on a human level,

With never a sense of personification,
Of realisation.
Never.
Purely - demoralisation.

Debbie Smith

I DON'T CARE TO BE A CARER

because the pay is crap.
Still you get to work from home
so will always be on tap.

Don't ask the hours required -
there's none set down you know:-
go to bed before daylight breaks
get up before cock crow.

Demands on your time limited
to twenty four hours a day.
No qualifications needed
as you're not entitled to pay.

No need to apply for a vacancy
should someone need the care
the job is immediately yours
with no chance of doing a job share.

Bill Picksley

TWO LUMPS

A lump developed recently:
The surgeon cut it out.
My throat was stitched, I went away
Healthy again no doubt.

A second lump came up last week
While waiting at Heathrow.
My golden opportunity and -
I didn't want to go.

The sights and sounds of Bristol:
My breeding and my birth,
My friends, my family, my life
Will haunt me still in Perth.

"Last call for QA one one two."
I swallow, board the plane.
Of these two lumps I know for sure
Which caused the greater pain.

Nick Moore

AS THE CROW FLIES

As the crow flies
his shadow darts across the uneven ground
lifting and sinking
over undulations and outcrops
stagnant pools and dry river beds
over red rock and dark earth.
He flies
over unsaid words and unwritten letters
ungrasped hands and unseeing eyes
over closed doors and unlived lives.
He pecks at the tightly-zipped bodybag
i drag behind me
and brings to light things
i had forgotten
or did not know
or did not want to know.
He alights
on my left shoulder
and i can see the iridescence
in his glassy black feathers
and the curved reflection of
my face in his fierce eye.
As the crow flies
he tilts his head and swings
his black blood-specked razor-beak
to my gaze, and winks at me
in a familiar way.

Paul Coade

THE DISTURBING TRANQUILLITY
OF SOLITUDE

In this ear-piercing silence
I'm surrounded by memories and walls
Slow motion pictures spinning and spiralling
Crazy images threatening and conspiring to swallow up
And dismember my past

.... if only
If only if only I could be back

Feeling the night thaw and watching the seconds stretch
Peering through the glass
Across the tranquil still waters of Hollow ponds
And the inviting sky a mixture of pinks and blues
Dancing on the ripples with the retreating moon
Dawn erupts into a slow crescendo of colour
And sound
Not of moorhen nor of coot
But of hobnailed boot and jangling keys
Of dog barking
Of deep rough northern voices guffawing and laughing
As the sounds of my reality seep through
The iron door to remind me of the life
I should be living

My thoughts and my fears
Drift to D Wing where grey-haired men
With black-eyed budgies pace and wait for a lifetime
To pass
Where the only hope is a letter from a friend
Or better yet a nuclear wipeout
A new clear way out

The magic mushroom cloud
To relieve the responsibility and devour the guilt
In one foul swoop
Up up up and away
Maybe not
Maybe just one well-aimed warhead would do the trick
But then again....... maybe not

Drift Paul Drift
Try to think of nicer things

Block out the bark and the shallow-minded laughter
Take yourself back
To a happy ever after
Like the time in Northeye in '85 when we rioted
For a fortnight razing the prison to the ground
Remember the satisfying sound of the northern
Hobnails retreating under a media glare
Every dog has its day and I'm glad I was there
But even now it doesn't compare to those nights
In waders wading waist high
Leaking and squelching through icy cold
Eerie black water to where the carp hides
And the tense tench bubbles rise
To cast my first cast of the new fishing season
Nights of rivers and lakes
Rhythms and reason
Hallucinogenics and acts of treason against the norm
But now
As the hobnails approach it seems the best I can do
Is pick up "The Profession of Violence"
And put down "The Tao of Pooh"

The Cutter

WHITE LINE RADIO

Charlie taught me everything I know
but now that I've learned, he won't let go
he wants to be the star of the show
and feed on me, and grow and grow
I said to Charlie, "Leave me alone"
but he just stares at me and my heart turns to stone
as he whispers, "Remember everything I've shown
you is real, and I gave you everything that you own."
Then Charlie sneers, "I'm against every law,
I'm the rich man's friend, gonna make you poor
I'm gonna rub some salt in your sore
You'd better believe it, I'm gonna make sure
that you suffer for all that you've ever done wrong
and you can't exorcise me by writing a song
a letter, a poem, a rant or a rage
and it's nothing to do with your job, or your age,
because I am your keeper
and you are in my cage."

And I wonder sometimes if Charlie is right
and it's me that's been wrong trying to keep up this fight
have I been blinded by his white light?
Or is he the saviour in all of his might, the power, the glory,
seated on the right hand of God?

But he can't be...
and then again,
he just might.

Adrian Lloyd

WAITING

I am waiting for the time
When the waiting stops
And the facade drops
When lies are things that others tell
And I can call when you're unwell.
I am waiting for the time
When nights are calm
And cause no harm
To those close by
As in your loving arms I lie.
I am waiting for the time
When the guilt has gone
And the crying's done
When all our hopes and dreams are real
And all we feel is what we feel
I am waiting for the time.

Tim Gibbard

THIS IS THE MILLENNIUM CALLING EARTH

This is the Millennium calling Earth, are you ready?
I saw women encamped on Greenham Common
And I watched as the tools of the apocalypse withdrew from my land.
I lived through the introduction of archaic tax laws
And I was there when the people of this country
Protested them into extinction.
I have seen the once impregnable castle of conservatism
Dashed upon the rocks of public opinion
And for the first time since it has been important to me
I have seen new overseers elected to govern my home.
I have seen free elections in South Africa
And the release of one of its greatest sons.
I watched as the people of Berlin
Wrestled the building blocks of segregation to the ground with their bare hands
And I have seen the freshly turned soil in the Gardens of Democracy
Made ready for us to plant for our future.
I have seen treaties signed on the world stage,
Promises and securities made.
I have seen continents meet in space,
Once alone behind Iron Curtains
Now standing together on the edge of a new unknown.
I have seen the fist of anger open into the hand of welcome
Its fingers reading new cultures like Braille.
I have gathered with 1,000 good citizens under the threat of imprisonment
Simply because we wanted to party.
I have met with 20,000 peacefully in the same place
Simply because we wanted to dance.
I have seen a city of 100,000 rise like Atlantis from the fields of Somerset,
Thrive and disperse in the space of a week
And I know that community is possible.
I have watched people lie down in the path of bulldozers,
Climb trees to protect them,
Tackle contractors with chainsaws.
I have seen people living in holes in the ground

Because they believe that the life-span of our green space
Is more important than the time it takes by the most direct Tarmac route
Between point A and point B
And I have seen friends of this planet frighten national governments
To the point of violent and explosive retaliation.
I have seen a growing understanding and acceptance of the need for conservation,
The cultivation of sustainable crops,
The recycling of materials,
Direct solar power used for heating, lighting and transport
And I have seen wind turbines spinning in the fields of England.
I have seen a return to natural religions,
An awareness of balance
And the rebuilding of a relationship with our environment and its life
That we lost when we started to believe that we knew what we were doing.
I have seen every facet of this glittering gem on which we live
Flash before my eyes in the safety of my own living room
And I now speak to those on its far side
As easily as I speak to you today
As I've seen the miles in between
Turned into a millionth of a second of data transmission.
I have seen doors opened, answers given, understanding gained,
Conclusions reached, wisdom evolved, love professed.
I have been out into this world and it is real
And I have returned with a world that will now
Virtually fit into my pocket.
I now know people who live on the far side of this planet.
I have friends who live on the far side of this planet.
I love people who live on the far side of this planet.
I have seen my world shrink to the size of my hands
And as I turn it slowly,
Feeling its damp clouds,
Dipping my fingers into its oceans,
Tickling my palms with its mountains and forests,
I see the insignificance of any thought that does not consider
Our responsibility to this beautiful creation.
I look out into a brilliant sky on the darkest night
And I force myself to consider just for an instant

The distance between us and the nearest stars
And between them and the next and so on
As they lie glimmering somewhere near our dawn
And I start to wonder what messages they may send tomorrow
And I start to wonder if there really is other life out there
And if there is are we ready to receive it
And if we are ready will it come
And then I start to think about how sad it would be
If it did come and we weren't here any more
And then I know that I am ready.
This is the Millennium calling Earth, are you ready?

Mike George
hello aliens

hello aliens is there anybody out there are you picking up our signals do
     you understand?
we are scanning through the universe for signs of your existence
hello aliens is there anybody out there are you picking up our signals
     please respond

we are sending you a picture of our galaxy our solar system
we are sending you a picture of the people of our planet so you'll know
     that we are friendly
hello aliens is there anybody out there are you picking up our signals do
     you understand?

we are sending you this capsule with some DNA some hydrogen some
     dust some rocks some molecules of carbon
we are sending you this capsule with some books of facts and formulas
     the product of a thousand generations
hello aliens is there anybody out there are you picking up our signals
     please respond

we have technology to make new forms of life intelligent computers and
     machines to reach the stars
we have technology to make new forms of death intelligent computers
     and machines to fight our wars
hello aliens is there anybody out there are you picking up our signals do
     you understand?

we believe if we had access to your scientific knowledge we could
     understand the meaning of the cosmos
we believe if we had access to your scientific knowledge we could learn
     the secrets of controlling time and space
hello aliens is there anybody out there are you picking up our signals
     please respond

we are scanning through the universe

we are probing every constellation for some sign of your existence

hello aliens is there anybody out there are you picking up our signals do
you understand?

hello aliens is there anybody out there are you picking up our signals
please respond

Nick Moore

SURFER

"There's an alien in the shower!"

its crimson torso
black arms and legs
head invisible
stands there
thin and lank
relaxed;

salt spray melts
into the swirling nebula
at its non-existent feet;

its inner being watches
from the steaming bath.

Gary Seabrook

WIBBLE A LITTLE, WOBBLE A LOT

Welcome to wibbly wobbly land
A profusion of confusion you can never understand
Where commuters commute to compute on their hands
And dazzling white horses turn cartwheels in the sand
Cats and dogs bounce around on spring-loaded tails
Past racecourses alive with the thunder of snails
Transportation in boats with multicoloured sails
Or riding on the spray of backwards whales
The ground and the air have no meeting places
And the sun and the clouds have big smiley faces
Analytically analysed a world of Feng Shui
Of translucence, transparence all softness and gooey
Purity, beauty and loving reactions
Making two halves one whole in one squashy fraction.

Debby Court

THE OSCILLATING ALSATION

Ooh, it's so exciting,
life's so much fun,
shall I chew my ass,
or go for a run,
chase a cat, or lie in the sun?

HEY! PUPPY! that's my food,
to stick your head in is really rude,
snarl, show my teeth,
then roll over,
let him bite me underneath.

When will pack leader get home from the pub?
When will pack leader give my tummy a rub?
Hark to the song of the dog..........
HOWL~
bet that made them jump,
now I'll bark at the door,
make the boss feel a chump
when she looks, to see that there's nothing there,
and I prance away with my tail in the air.

I like chasing cats,
that's lots of fun,
I bark really loud
and watch them run.
Throw the ball! Throw the ball!!
Just throw the goddam ball!!!
What's this? a bath?
don't make me laugh,
we'll have to fight if you want me in there,
go on I dare you, oh shit, she does dare!

I'm all wet now,
like a bedraggled rat,
I smell of shampoo,
and my fur's all flat.

SHAKE....

Now there's water, water everywhere
and not a drop on me,
excuse me while I scratch my ear,
I think I've found a flea.

I'm so fucking hard
when I BITE the vacuum cleaner,
but the way it growls
you would think it thinks it's meaner than me.
Hah! we'll soon see
when I go on the attack,
knock it clean on its back,
and hope I don't get got
by the electricity.

I'm Attilla the Hound
and with a leap and a bound
I'll joyously greet you
'cos I'm so pleased to meet you
I'm Attilla the Hound.

Mike George

NO DOG NO MORE

Ain't got no dog
No more

No walk no dog
No talk no dog
No teach no dog no tricks
No more

Ain't got no dog
No more

No dog no run
No dog no jump
No dog no chase no sticks
No more

Ain't got no dog
No more

Dog died

Avril Staple

LOST PROPERTY

Excuse me please - has anyone seen my sense of humour?
I had it before my washing machine broke down and my dole was cut.
It was sort of roundish, had a big smile and was a bit off the cuff.
I put it down somewhere because it kept being misunderstood.
I've looked under the bills in the empty cupboards
and amongst the pile of rubbish in the garden.
I thought I might have put it in my diary
but that was only full of important things.
I've checked with my friends
but they said they hadn't seen it for ages
and in the DSS office, they said they would look into it.
It wasn't in Kwik Save or the launderette.
I thought of applying for a loan
but where do you go to for that sort of thing?
I saw one just like it on the TV.
I reckon someone nicked it when I was in the pub.
It might be in the medicine cabinet next to the Valium.
I know I had it because there are pictures of it in the photo album.
Knowing me I've probably put it somewhere safe.
You have to look after these things you know
because when life gets really tough
a sense of humour is the best friend you've got.

Mark C

WHEN I WAS A LAD

Hartcliffe, that lovely place where I was born
One shitty, fucked up council estate, battered and torn
We were bored, we were pissed off, we had fuck all to do
But that all changed, when we found the joys of sniffing glue

Evo Stick, Evo Stick, Evo Stick

Oh God man, that stuff was just amazing shit
Hardware stores, that's where we stole our glue
Great Mills, Do It All, B & Q
To get there we took and drove away
Fast cars, key up jobs, thieved the easy way
Mark Two Escort, RS 2000
Headcase glue sniffers driving like Nigel Mansell
We looked odd, we stuck out, but we didn't give a shit
Cos all we wanted was our

Evo Stick, Evo Stick, Evo Stick

On the way there, "Hey man, blend in, drive slow..."
Going home, different story, foot to the floor, "Go man go!"
Four 13 year old kids, gasping, in need of a sniff
In a rush, to get back home, to good old Hartcliffe
"Fuck!" Blue lights in the mirror, police up your ass
110 mph, "Fuck you coppers, you'll have to do better than that,"
Tyres screeching, back wheels spinning, "you ain't catching us
Cos that pile of shit you're driving just ain't fast enough!"
Park it up, set it alight, we're not getting nicked
Cos we're all off to have a sniff of

Evo Stick, Evo Stick, Evo Stick

Quick time lads, on your toes, let's leave this burning shell
But don't forget the can of petrol, cos we can sniff that as well

Emel

COPS AND ROBBERS

Turn off your mind, turn on your telly
Animated society of frightfully shiny type people
Dolby stereo type people
Wide screened white teeth type people
Muscley chinned heroes fighting evil
Cops in flaired chinos chasing Negroes in stolen cars
Buy a Mars, it will help you work rest and play
Play, play in the infested big breasted scenes
'Congratulations Mrs. Nobody
You've just won yourself a washing-machine
Would you like to gamble on the holiday in the Bahamas?'
We'll all step back from these mellow dramas
So turn off your emotions and turn on your tellies
Watch your Gardening Programmes, put on your virtual wellies
Cos our kids are selling their souls
To the dreaded game consoles
Learning how to kill their enemies with guns and lasers
Your sister screaming in your face because you forgot to tape Neighbours.

So are our lives conducted by TV's routines?
Or do we just enjoy watching our dreams?
Or is it a form of electric relaxation?
Or is it a big blonde blockbuster bazooka blowing
hair flowing politically correct special effect space monster
disaster vampire type flick?

So turn on your mind, turn off your telly.

Rob Cookson

BOLLOCKS

The pool table pops
as the juke box bops
I hear the crowded conversation at the bar
and laughter rocks
as men in white socks
eye pretty girls in
                          summer frocks

There's a hippie that loves us lots
with his brother in dreadlocks
there's two lads in headlocks
somebody call the cops
                          pillocks

An old man mocks
for nothing he sees shocks

I can see a loner in padlocks
women dressed like peacocks
and the local girl that
                          sucks cocks

I feel like we are all props
in different scenes and backdrops
while some audience claps
                          Bollocks.

Jasper Hardhat

FREETIME BRO

freetime brother
the road runs on ahead
the rain comes down heavy
and there's no-one up ahead
ahhh the city has
a heart without a love
and there ain't no knowing
when I'm going to get close
to that which is up above
now the lights flick through
from amber to green
so hang on brother
twist that throttle wide
hit the highway
and
ride

John Kandinsky

CRASH
(For: a boy killed on his nineteenth birthday)

I think too much sometimes.
Recalling things
(lots of things)
that do me no good.
I drag them out
from wherever they live,
things better left where they are.

It's an old game this running
and re-running
over and over again.
Things that will do me no good.
And I don't know why I do it.

I am recalling now...
a warm autumn night
outside of some pub.
A dock-side pub.
Talking poetry
copyright,
opportunities,
and bollocks.

And all of us
in too much of a hurry,
too much of a rush
to get somewhere,
anywhere
and be known
and be famous
and be recognised

but it was all
so much
small beer.

There were the final
"good-nights".
A last glance.
And the oil
and water mixed,
catching and reflecting
the lights of those bars.

It could have been blood.
Because blood, oil and water
all look the same
in the dark.
And it was all,
all of it,
so much small beer.

You?
You were leaving your pub.
Nineteen that day.
Out of your mind,
shit-faced and unreasonable.
No talk of poetry in your crowd.
You were making
statements
of
managing your car
managing your beer
managing your life
when you couldn't even
manage yourself.

You took out some wall.

I saw you go,
wheels in the air
leaping that central
reservation,
and both of you
were in there
flying in the air.

I wrenched at
your door.
You were both
curled like kittens
on the front seat
of that beat-up
Ford.

And there was oil
and blood
and water
and it all looked
the same
in the dark.

I reached in,
took a handful
of you,
and pulled you out of
that car.

And I felt your throat,
and there was nothing,
there was nothing
where there should have
been something.
Not even a flicker
of you.

Where were you?
Did you see us
wherever you were?
Did you see
when I gave you the air
I could hardly afford?
My heartbeat was yours
if you'd asked,
a birthday gift
from me to you.

I thumped down hard
and knocked on your chest,
and for a second or two,
one glorious second or two,
your eyes flicked up,
your pulse came in
and you did come back.
Yes, you did come back.
And all of us thought...
'we're in business.'
The business of
getting you back.

That happened twice.
Twice you came back.
The third time
you never did.
Not even the experts
could find where
you'd gone.

And the green sheets hung
and I knew,
I knew you were gone

and that
was not small beer
to me.

Your death
touched my life,
it diminished me more
than I can say.
Someone I never knew
did all that...
to me.

I shall never pass here...
without thinking of
that night
that poetry
those lights
and all of that water
oil and blood in the dark
and you...
who never came back
not even...
for me.

Lorraine Pickles

CATCHING TRAINS

I ordered a taxi and got a unicorn.
The man was very apologetic -
All the cabs were booked
Some kind of business conference.
I explained I had a train to catch
As I heaved myself upon the unicorn's back
His mane and haunches smelling of the sea.

The unicorn was quite chatty
Said he hated picking up drunks
And impolite people with lots of luggage.
I didn't ask him to stop at your house
But he elevated himself sufficiently
So I could peer into your upstairs window.
You were asleep, so I banged on the glass
"Come back," I said,
"It's all been a terrible mistake,"
But you didn't wake up.

He pointed out, not unkindly
That we had a train to catch.
I didn't ask him to stop at my house
But there, through the upstairs window
I saw myself, a child again
Wandering from dream to dream
Years away from draughty platforms.
"Come back," I said,
"It's all been a terrible mistake."

The unicorn frowned in a disapproving way
As if to say this wasn't the way to catch trains.

We came then to the station
He inclined his horn slightly as I left.
I watched him, through the glass
Having a fag at the taxi rank.

I missed the train, of course.
Too much hanging around windows.

Nigel Pearce

INSTALLATION INSTRUCTIONS
FOR ARTISTIC PERSONALITY
VERSION 7.5

Unplug your eyes from their sockets if accessible. If unable to unplug the
eyes, change the spinal cord with the eyes still in situ.

Turn your life upside down by releasing your friends from the retainer,
place your family to one side. Go for long walks, learn to read the tide.

Replace friends with a book, music and studio space. If you don't have
access to a studio, just rename a room you're familiar with.

Obtain a lover who is strange and challenges everything you believe in. In
its normal position let him plug in, and smoke lots of rollies.

Lights will flash after a few days, this will stop and the correct things to
say will appear on the LC display, experiment, think, maybe you're the
new funk rebel leader.

Start by being quiet and observing things. To prevent damage you must
not open the back of your thoughts with the imagination turned on.
Having an unusual dress code is optional. Live skilfully, suffer for your
cause and communicate.

You can determine whether your artistic system 7.5 is causing family and
friends frequency interference by asking them. You may want to show the
system 7.5 life artistic rights and guarantee.

If you encounter any problems please contact your Inner Voice Adviceline
on expensive phone 0800 0117 3 who will provide assistance as required.

Henry Lawrence

THE ULTIMATE CRAP TECHNO SONG

I thought I heard the ultimate crap Techno song the other day
a dreary drum machine was clicking over a distorted bass
but worse than that was what was happening on the vocal line
this anorak was whingeing about installing Windows 95.

I'd thought I'd heard it all by now, but no, I must have got it wrong
I'd thought they'd plumbed the depths with what could ever be described as song
but here was something worse than all that junk the kids get into
this rapper had a problem setting up a Postscript™ printer.

My ears began to flap in time, my soul began to retch
I was pretty much convinced that Armageddon happened next
I looked about for any hopeful avenue of escape
and then I saw him at the bar, chatting to his mate.

For once the mix was perfect, and I for one was fooled
there was no real vocal track, conversation ruled
propeller heads discussed the problems of their SCSI drives
at a hundred and twenty beats per minute, perfectly synchronised.

OOH BABY ENERGY

Yo, Yo, Yo, what's up?
Word up!
My name's Tina T,
Otherwise known as Tasty.
I'm lead voguealist in the new slop sexation
That's sleeping across the nation at the moment.
You know The Spunk Girls.
I'd just like to say that I'm very proud to be a part,
Hee-hee, get it, apart?
Of the biggest,
Ooh baby energy, fleecing spree
For anyone to see happen this millennium.
There's 5 of us in the band
And I play with,
Hee-hee, play with?
Mels A, B and C and Natali G Spot.
Otherwise known as
Loadsa, Easy, Juicy and Hot Spunk
Because we're not very young, posh or sporty really.
We all agree it's lovely to be top of the tarts
And would like everyone to believe
That we take our positions of responsibility very seriously.
Although personally,
I actually prefer the missionary
Or from behind.
Anyway, my favourite drink is Hooch
Or any of the other drinks made for kids.
I'll have a slow comfortable screw later
And my favourite game
Is Remembering Your Last Boyfriend's Name.
Hee-hee, Easy always gets it wrong.
She has trouble with her own last name sometimes.

We only ever,
Hee-hee, tackle all the big issues.
Like the colour of our hair,
What's best not to wear
And did he have velvety, soft, quilted tissues in his bathroom.
Can we sing in tune
And do we really care.
You can see us regularly on TV
Or daily as near to page 3 as we can be
In your papers.
We would like to remind everybody
Who hasn't already obscene us
That we are currently whoring all over the place.
So don't worry,
We will be coming in an area near you soon.
So boys, sweet dreams,
Keep your willies clean,
And girls, keep your eyes open
As well!
And when you do see us
Don't burst a vessel if you scream.
This is me, Tina T, saying,

                              Ooh baby energy everybody!

                    Goodbye. XXX.

Nigel Pearce
DISCO

An occasion at which typically young people dance to amplified
pop records, usually compered by a disc jockey and featuring
special lighting effects.
You can find me down the local discotheques.

So you were feeling central and just lost it there,
gave it up and didn't care,
standing cool like close-ups in Super-8.
Who are the ones you rate?
It's touch to touch,
fingertip stuff,
equal with the people on a floor in parallel.
Here we sell

flowers with kerosene.
You dance obscene,
like reckless I mean.
Your funk is great,
you dance and gyrate
(and is that your mate?)
to the beat,
skin moves,
look up,
love me,
I exist.
And a couple of drinks plus two is four,
Come on there's a love law,
I've gotta dance with you,
I wanna explore,
give it to me
I want more more more.

I'm an experienced groover
and you're a super mover.
I'm working on your rhythm,
thinking what to give 'em.
I'll raise my arm and hold it high,
not too fast, make it last,
I'll bring it down real slow...
finger pointed like a gun, close to body,
we're together like Big Ears and Noddy.

They're playing some of my favourite alcohol hits,
the track 'Unfinished Sympathy' Massive Attack,
'Walk On' Smith and Mighty,
then disco with Sister Sledge, the song 'Thinking Of You'
opening line:
everybody let me tell you 'bout my love,
brought to me by an angel from above...
Then Curtis Mayfield, he's so positive,
remember *tomorrow is a brand new day,*
Roy Ayers 'Running Away':
do be do run run run
do be do run run run
'Le Freak' Chic,
then up-to-date with the Fila Brazilia mix of 'Cotton Wool' by Lamb,
and I know the DJ Sam,
alright, respect, wicked man..... yeah.

Forget that cool bit on the side and the joint,
I'm going to the middle, the focal point.
The crowd parts as we walk to the centre
(and I hope she remembers the money I lent her)
We cross arms, link and spin,
darkness is lit by a disco globe,
hundreds of moving light dots
come to life on other people's tops.

It's Abba 'Dancing Queen' -
Disc Jockey, play me my favourite line!
Get closer this time...
see that girl,
watch that scene,
digging the dancing queen.

Disco Woman, how much have you discoed?
You can disco yourself now and dance on your own.

Anyway here's my number, please give me a phone....
.....

Martyn Hudson
VINYL JUNKIE

I'm a vinyl junkie
Looking to score
CDs don't do it
Nor tapes anymore
They're both not-so-cheap imitations
Of the original high fidelity creation

Tapes stretch and snap
CDs skip, records scratch
I too know that itch
If I don't find my fix

Going to see a dealer
To check out what he's got
Plenty of suppliers
Who'll feed this need
All of them smiling
And willing to please

Don't care what clothes I wear
It's a luxury to eat
Craving that tribal beat
I like my vinyl medium rare
As long as it's rock
I don't really care
I've a preference for the hard stuff
But no amount is ever enough

Hip-hop, Techno, Rap
Blasphemous crap
To finely tuned ears
Abomination by dilution
Technological tricks
Distorted in the mix
Inbred, commercially fed
Are all real musicians dead?

I don't need any status
As long as I have my stylus
Through the needle
I get satisfaction
Going round in circles
With my plastic passion

I'm a vinyl junkie, losing the plot
I'm a vinyl junkie, I just can't stop
I'm a vinyl junkie-.......... junkie-.......... junkie-..........
junkie-.......... junkie-.......... junkie-

Lucy English

HIPPY CHICK

I'm a hippy chick and proud of it
so, don't give me any of your lies
like, I'm untogether and I'm unclean
and I'm a mess   I'm not   because I wear old jeans
doesn't mean I haven't got a future
doesn't mean I haven't got a vision
I can see through your lies
New Labour is danger, now that's a lie
and if you believe the government
then I'll think you're a total policeman.
You're repressed   You're regressed
You're obsessed   with control
but you can't control my mind.
I've got an active, floating, wired up brain
can't you see I'm completely involved
with improving my higher self?   I'm not on the shelf
you won't find me working in a bank
but you might find me in bed having a cheese sandwich
and reading poetry and working things out
like how did it all start
I mean the universe, and this planet?
I want to know, I want to show you
I want to reclaim a whale. I want to save a street.
I want to find the place where heaven meets earth.
I'm searching, I'm stretching my thoughts
I'm connecting to my environment
I'm listening to the Red Hot Chilli Peppers and Nirvana
I'm smoking home grown marijuana
but my mind is totally clear.
      Wow it's all happening here.
Let me tell you   I'm the dippy trippy hippy   that's what you see
but inside I'm only concerned with
my love of humanity.

It's a manic world we're living in.
Manic people and too many dustbins
full of rubbish.   We should be recycling.
We should be inviting ourselves to a tribal party
and sharing resources,   because the world is alive
and wide
and I've only seen a part of it
and I want to see more.
I want to travel around this world
like a sailing ship   with my sails unfurled
like a speeding car   like a speeding plane
I told you before   I'm completely concerned
with improving myself.
I'm into outer space   I'm into emotions
I want to dissolve the boundaries between me and you
and I want to   and I want to...
dump you because you're in my way
you're blocking my growth.   I want to say
you're a guy who's on the dole
and I'm a hippy chick with a goddess soul.
You're going nowhere and I'm flying.
I'm re-inventing myself and you're not trying
to improve.
You're static   You're tiny   You're a dot
You're a walk-on part in Act 2 scene three
and I'm The Script.   I'm The Play   and I'm writing it
and you're afraid of me.
Did you think I would turn back the clock?
Did you think I would suck you dry?
You're the guy who's down on his luck
and I'm the hippy chick who needs a
damn   good   deal   of   space.

Julie Boston

TOURIST INFORMATION

LEISURE SUPPLIED
IN THE COUNTRYSIDE

BIRD WATCHERS
PARK 'N' HIDE

BALLOONISTS
PARK 'N' GLIDE

RAMBLERS
PARK 'N' STRIDE

SKIERS
PARK 'N' SLIDE

FAMILIES
PARK 'N' DIVIDE

LOVERS
PARK 'N' CONFIDE

OVERNIGHT
PARK 'N' ABIDE
WITH LEISURE
SUPPLIED
IN THE COUNTRYSIDE

Jeremy Dixon

PARKING

Once
Late at night
On my way home
In the park
A man asked if I had the time
I did

Sheldon King

THE PEDESTRIAN

I'm a pedestrian me, see
no number
plates of meat
me
on the corner
shop soiled, not oiled and boil in the bag,
cat's out
and so am I
ching ching
goes the conductor of the bustling bus
stop
what a con
ducked a wing of a....
plain speech?
not likely on yer bike
get cycley
crikey
bit of a major thud of the future that
nearly left me flat
broke my white collar
bone shaking workaholic neck
still not one red cent
from heaven
pennies farthing
further than ever this year
more like red neck
(plenty of that)
mine's on the white line, marking
time, piece of mine
shafted
should have stuck out my
thumb nail sketch book

look........listen
and when no cars
Flash (the green man)
Gordon Bennett (Defender of the Universe)
leadeth me
and feedeth me
on bread and quiet water,
take me home to your geodesic dome
where sheep may safely
butt, Rome wasn't built in a day
no way
not with Nero fiddling the books
burning bridges
selling fridges
and he's not alone
after all, when in Rome
all roads lead to
all roads are paved with
golden shower curtained corruption
all roads bleed (menstrual cycles)
wheeler dealer peddles whatever
clever
meanwhile I look right
left
bereft of my shoe leather
no soul
just cobblers drive a nail
into my coughing fit,
for nothing doing
little feat.

Matt Black

THE PROBLEM OF CARPET

You've always wanted a carpet.
Now you've got a carpet.
Now you don't know if you want it.
You say what's the point of carpet?
You sound a bit like Samuel Beckett.
Would you rather your floor was parquet?
You say what's the point of parquet?
You say what's the point of floor?
It just takes you to the door.
You say what's the point of door?
It just takes you to more carpet.
You say what's the point of carpet?
It just goes from wall to wall.
Now do you want some carpet slippers?
What's the point of carpet slippers?
Now do you want to eat kippers?
In your carpet slippers on the carpet?
What's the point of kippers?
What's the point of nippers?
They play on the carpet.
I know that they like carpet.
Maybe they can't help it.
It's soft and they don't pay for it.
I know that I like carpet.
I'll have your carpet if you don't want it.
But think about it carefully.
You have always wanted a carpet.

Sarah Leedham-Green

THE SECOND LAW OF THERMODYNAMICS

My flat is ruled by gravity.
It silently obeys the second law of thermodynamics
So that only the astute would notice it.
I have noticed it.

I have seen my books once lofty
Move one by one from shelf to table to floor.
Discarded clothes lie like deflated bodies, bereft of energy,
It is all my jacket can do to stay on a chair,
Arms sagging over, waiting to fall.

Mugs no longer hang from racks
But malinger under sofas, beds, chairs, anywheres.
Cupboards have lost their meaning.
Even the plaster has started peeling from the ceiling,
I find thin fragments in my hair.

Sometimes I wonder how long it will be
Before my first floor flat sinks down to the ground floor,
Sometimes I wonder if it will be worth more?

It is getting dangerous.
Yesterday I trod on John Irving and apologised,
I have broken Dostoyevsky's spine
Slipped on a pair of knickers
And clumsily knocked over a hidden glass of red wine.

We are all slowly falling,
Moving downwards to our lowest state,
Losing energy.
I lie flat on my back to watch TV
And when friends come round
We lie together and slowly atrophy.

Pete Brown

THE SCANDAL
OF MODERN BUILDING REGULATIONS

The headboard was creaking
    and the girl was squealing
The bedsprings were squeaking
    cracks appeared in the ceiling
and plaster fell to the floor
The whole house was shaking
    and still she cried out for more
Her cries got faster and louder
    the air was thick with displaced plaster powder
- And then - "Oh my God" - she came
    like a cross between a train - and a frightened sheep
"Oh God" she cried - thank God I thought
    - maybe now we can get some sleep
    For there was no pleasure in it for me, you know
Oh no - we were trying to sleep - in the flat below
    and we had to go to work in the morning
- Already Monday morn was dawning
    and we hadn't slept a wink all night
We were knackered -
Shagged out - from upstairs' sexual appetites

Well I gave Clare an understanding hug
    and she gave me a brave little kiss
And we both agreed - that we couldn't be doing with this

At first we had laughed - when they did their thing
    listening to the yelps and whimpers
    and watching the lampshade swing
But it'd been going on for over a fortnight now
    We'd been pleased for Rich at first
but now we hated him - and his noisy little cow

Because this lack of sleep - was beginning to bite deep
    and making us touchy and grumpy
We were wired - and far too tired
for our own - more gentle form - of adult rumpy-pumpy
    And this took its toll - on me especially
as I couldn't help thinking about Clare and me
    and what if she compared me sexually
    with that stallion up the stair
Christ, how could I compare - in the trouser department
with the 3-times-a-night man - in the penthouse apartment
    And I wondered - Did Clare
    lie awake all night listening
    imagining their bodies, wet and glistening
    Wishing that it were she
upstairs - in all those oh so noisy throes of abandoned ecstasy
    Wishing that it were Rich instead
of me - who lay beside her in our bed?
    Was Clare - lying there
    imagining Richard rogering
envying - the girl who'd Richard's todger in
    and wondering
if she should ask the upstairs' lodger in
    'For a coffee' - when I'm out?
    - Such terrible fears and doubts -
Magnified by lack of sleep - such scary thoughts dig deep
I know that I should share - these thoughts with Clare
    and trust her
But the truth is that I'm just too scared to dare
    Because I love her
and can't bear to think of her thinking
    of the man one floor above her
    Because it hurts
Meanwhile   on the other side of the bed
Clare   who can't bear to listen to upstairs
    pulls the duvet over her head - and thinks
    about that noisy little minx - and how she can't compare

with 18 year old skin - and never dyed hair
    And how, maybe
she should make more of an effort
    in her own love-making
Go hell-for-leather - with more groans, and more faking
    And she wonders - if Pete's got bored with her
because since that girl moved in - he hasn't even pawed at her
    And she can tell - that he's got something on his mind
    That something's up - and it isn't Pete.

Glenn Carmichael

SEX

SEX!
Well slide some skin on me.
Of course I like it,
I like what you do to me.

No, I can't say it
(But you know that it's true)
There's people here,
I can't say, "I love you."

Give me your sex;
Give it me please.
You know that I'm hungry;
I'm down on my knees.
You've locked the door,
So now give me the keys!
I'll just get a rubber...
I don't want no disease.
Here, put on this rubber suit,
Grab this and squeeze.

God, your sex feels good to me.
I'm riding that horse,
And I'm wild and I'm free.
Everything's buzzing,
Even the beez-zz-zz...
When you say, "Sex?"
I say, "Yes, please!"

I don't want no distractions,
I haven't a clue.
You're the materials,
I'm just the glue.

Of course I'd believe you
If you said black was blue
(Oo-ooh!)
Give me your sex,
I like what you do.

I can remember
When sex was fun.
I'm sick of these war games,
Just give me a gun.
"I'm just passing thru dear."
That's love on the run.
Sex is for suckers...
Oops, pardon the pun.
Sexual rhythms go on...
and on... and on... and on...

Ah-chu... chu... chu... chu...
Chu - chu - chu - chu -
Wooh-hooh!
I'm a runaway train baby!
Comin' down your track!
(A-clickety-clack, a-clickety-clack)
And ahead is the tunnel...
Wooh-ooh!
Aa-ah - sh-sh-sh...
There's a light up ahead.

I am the doctor.
You're sexual healing.
I am the room
And you've got me reeling.
You are a dance
That we do on the ceiling.
I do know the words
But I forgot the meaning.

I am a story;
No end or beginning.
You are the tops
And I can't stop spinning.
I won't ask the question,
I don't care what comes next.
I stand with my vest on...
Please - give - me - some - **SEX!**

Alison Brumfitt

SEX AND DEATH

There are things that come back and back,
things that art is always made about,
they get labelled as great traditions,
they are the nation's great obsessions.

There seems to be a market for certain types of poetry.
People want poetry with a bit of melodrama,
a bit of humour, a lot of swearing,
sex, violence, that kind of thing.

What is it with sex and death?
That they dance like lovers into the grave.
Unfathomed and fascinating.
There's a lot of energy in sex, and death.
Then you burn it, burn it into explosion.
Of course you can have sex again,
death has taken every last drop,
it's the last party, will you come?
Will you lick up the last drop
until it's gone?

What is it with sex and death
that they keep your mind entangled always?
Sometimes opposites do attract.
The procreation and elimination thing,
the standing on the edge full of adrenaline.
Going over the edge and to the end.
You can crash over the threshold,
the final frontier, will you come?
Who do you want crashing on the threshold,
and which one?

This is an age of revolutions,
everywhere, everything, shock, shock, shocking.
Everybody's chasing liberation.
Now it's getting a bit boring.

People want the same thing over and over,
they're chasing some king of thrill.
It is getting, don't you think, a touch mundane,
making the same points over and over again.

Oh yeah, it's interesting, but it's not the only thing.
Is it the only thing for you right now?
Is it your only thing right now?
Is it anything now?

You could ask me to write a poem about sex and death,
you could do.
And I could tell you to fuck off and die,
I could do.

Kevin McKeigue

POSITIVE HIV

When they brought me from the hospital bed
Cold, alone, I sat upon the chair
I could see through the doctor's eyes
All hope for me was prayer
When they handed me the paper
My cries rang like a bell
But before I'd finished reading it
He began to cry as well
For the print upon that death warrant
Was so plain for me to see
A little tick beside those words
'Positive HIV'

I now face the greatest pain
Known to man
I'm going to die   I'm going to die
Yes I am

Unsafe sex, that's what I blame
It haunts my every move
My dying breath
Nobody knows the pain

Clean needles and condoms will protect us
At least that's what wise men all say
Take their advice, be real smart
Life - it's too high a price to pay
And when all my lifeless blood has gone
And back to dust I go
Remember man, protect yourself
Don't let this illness grow
This one is for our government
Forget your legislation
And give the kids in school what they need
In the name of God
Give them education

Rosalyn Chissick
Childhood Cancelled

Childhood cancelled due to lack of emotional funds.
We regret the inconvenience to those expecting
curiosity, wonder and fun, but limited resources
(due to parental handicap) mean that until further notice
children will have to assume adult responsibilities.

Christine Power
THE EXPERIENCE OF PARENTING

Lifelong training on the job

        with no recognition or salary

Appearing in court at every sitting

        a defendant in every crime

Being bound with bandages from head to foot

        then castigated for not moving

and smiling at deep wounds in your stomach.

Like Gulliver in his travels

a giant tied up by little people and

a tiny being surrounded by ogres

You are the victim of murder

        and the murderer too

High Priest and penitent parishioner

The experience of parenting is

      like being a child at a funfair

            on a whizzing round ride

                  which climbs and dips

giving views of the sea

        then pushes nose first to the ground

    spinning clockwise

            then anti-clockwise

and you that child

    screaming laughing feeling sick

        but

      knowing full well

    you just don't want it to stop.

Rosemary Gamsa

PLAYGROUND

Nighttime citybuzz
Streetlamp glare
Hide and seek
And who goes there?

Subway echo
Jungle Park
Everyone's a stranger
After dark.

Bus stop postbox
Endless wait
Time gets restless
Stay up late.

Cat's eye bushes
Curtained lace
Rustling wrappers
Paperchase.

Puddled gutters
Chains and locks
Cardboard castout
Jack in the box.

Red man danger
Green man cross
Long legged lycra
Candy Floss.

Knockout Ginger
Roundabout
Rusting dustbins
Let us out!

Sirens silence
Neon light
Shadow puppets
Prowl tonight.

Blindfold alley
Deadman's lane
Manhole rattle
Down the drain.

Drunks and poets
Déjà vu
Lovers killers
Who are you?

Chase me kiss me
Sharp edged air
Laugh too loudly
Truth or dare?

Up the ladder
Down the wall
What has happened
To us all?

Can't get in
They've locked the door...
                    Aren't we children any more?

Ursula Brooke

SUMMER 1997

MAY, all mud and roots, up to my neck in
blind growth which blots out all vision and imagination
as more and more emerging crowns
heave the earth open.

There's a trellis on the wall
a sitting duck for odd balls, footballs
and short cuts next door. A trellis
much knocked sideways, with tendrils
tightening their hold on it
making corkscrews
waving ropes and teams of ropes
to knit a new jersey for dilapidated diamonds.

In JUNE the church roof raised another fête.
It always could and should
with cups of tea for 50p
and Fairy cakes the same
no need for change.
The painted children's faces get
all bric-a-bracketed to sticky toys
beside which the jam scones are gone again
as we swat the rat and swat the rat, Amen

JULY walks to the barley field
through the wood
where black leaves make a ceiling against the sky
and dance there
like the sun's bunting.
Children yelp and dive through white lines of straw.
We, and the doctor, are drawn to chat
in the stubble.
We chat about straw.

In AUGUST, dressed in summer things
like shorts and slings
the wounded are steered
through Casualty
by next of kins.

Kieron's is a blanket.
He stands and sits all afternoon.
Reception asks "Is there a person
here with a dog bite?"
Kieron gets his tetanus and leaves.

Kieron comes back in
to sit
and stand
in Casualty, and I only know this because
I fell off my bicycle.

SEPTEMBER tea party
Better red than dead
Jeremiah said God said, and
here I am with Barbara Bigwood's
bread and butter tea cake.
I am where I am
and
doing what's happening
to the washing-up
in Babylonia which cannot be expressed in words.

Toby Farrow

THE WILD MUSHROOM PICKERS

Grandpa had hair on his head,
frost white curls that gleamed
in the sun
like aluminium.
He had a sit-on lawn mower
& every week I'd perch on his lap
wearing an old crash helmet,
so the roar became muffled
& my vision scratched.
With my eyes shut I felt like a spaceman
travelling to the moon.

Every year he drove around the streets
with a loudspeaker attached
to the roof of a yellow Jaguar.
When he spoke
his voice erupted
above our heads,
cracked into people's doors,
whipped & skittered off the tarmac.
When he spoke
I felt like God's apprentice.

When Mum went into hospital
I stayed with him.
He put me in red wellies
& we went into the fields
picking mushrooms bigger than plates.
Back home in the kitchen
with the swirly carpet
Grandma cooked them with eggs.

Side by side we sat &
simultaneously cut
into the fluted discs
then devoured the butter
dripping
through slats
onto our tongues.

When Mum got out of hospital,
I had a baby brother.

"What's he gardening for? He won't listen to a word
the doctor says. Won't listen to a word anyone says,
just being bullish, doing his own thing like he always does"

At what point do words that mean nothing
turn into words that mean everything?

The day before Cub Camp
Grandpa taught me how to say Bonjour,
but not goodbye.
One week later I returned
full of tales of giant killer eels.
Mum & Dad were bleary on the stairs,
wrapped in white dressing gowns
like shrouds.

At the funeral the Church felt like a sow
full to the brim
with live things.
When they put the box in the car
I stood next to
my brother and cousins
and we all cried
as if someone had pressed a button.
When the car drove off I imagined
there was a megaphone on the roof
& I almost heard thunder.

Sometimes I still feel him fleetingly
brushing my feet
in dewy fields
fresh
in rich continental sauce,
washed down with wine,
warm and safe at family suppers
or mopped in ketchup as a hangover cure.

At times like these,
I remember my red boots
& his basket of mushrooms,
& lament that
though I learned "Bonjour"
I never said "Goodbye."

Keith Davey

And the snow kept falling....

When she ate the cigarette ends one by one, well we started to worry
But brushed it aside with feigned indifference.
And the snow drops floated down upon the lawn....

Dad just joked that it was "old-timer's" disease
And kept his tears hidden along with her pills.
And the snow slowly covered the ground....

When she asked after Ethel we said she was fine
And lied guiltily, remembering her funeral long, long ago.
And the snow carefully covered the grass....

When I said "come on Mum" and her eyes looked not at me
But at someone strange, someone from long ago.
And the snow blurred the edges of the path....

When Dad gently took her hand she pushed him away
Saying that she was perfectly alright, she just wanted to sleep.
And the garden was a white blur, with a few shades of grey.

All around was an expanse of whiteness
Shapes, patterns, forms buried
All was white.... with a tint of grey
And the snow kept falling....

Lesley Anne Rose

THE SEANCE

To entertain the lethargic eternity
Of an airless afternoon,
Grandmother shuffled out her family photos.
Animated by musty pride,
She shared sepia faces
Whose staring eyes held shadows of my own.

"You've your great-grandmother's glorious hair,
And the nose of Uncle Albert I swear,
Eyes from your father, perfect sight on our side."

Too bored to disguise disinterest,
I was flirting with adolescence,
And allowing arrogance to test its wings.

Suddenly a fresh photograph revealed its face,
Lifting the old,
"That's your mother's youngest cousin -
Just finished 'A' levels, nice lad I'm told."

Nice lad! I saw Adonis in your smile,
Hands contorted in Levi pockets,
Your cocky, self-conscious squint requested devotion.
My heart blushed,
Distressed by a different beat,
And short-sighted eyes burnt with awe.

Now, much older, I patronise this adolescent,
And although still arrogant in Grandmother's house,
Infatuation and innocence were not so faithful.

And yet there has not been a single subsequent visit
To that unaltered, still stuffy home,
That I haven't combed cupboards,
Explored drawers, and inquired of every nook and cranny.
Searching for a photograph - searching for a feeling,
Once more waiting with the dead: Hidden: Not forgotten.

Jessica d'Este
INSTRUCTION

Do you wish
To be a poet?
I shall tell you
How to do it.

First you listen
Then you reach
For Sense and Rhythm
Before you speak.

No trouble, really
Truly, no
If you follow
What you truly know:

No trouble, really
Because what you Know
Doubles what you Feel
And grows

From all you Touch
And See and Taste
Sometimes Good
Sometimes Base -

As in all the din
Becoming Song
Because Life is short
And Art is long

It follows Joy
To full Expression
By rule of Clarity
Resolution

Truth is Beauty
All that matters:
A Surprise of Syntax
Rhyme and Clatter.

So there you are
A Poet be -
Lucid, Lucky
Truly Free.

Gill Higgins

DISPLACEMENT ACTIVITY

Write a poem for The Slam?
Really, I don't think I can...
I've got far too much to do...
Well... like drinking tea and going to the loo!
And watching Neighbours right through (Twice!)

I'm sure there's poems in my head...
But just right now, I'm off to bed.
It'll only be for an hour...
Then after that I'll have a shower.

But I really need my eyebrows plucked...
And ring that man I'd like to fuck!

So why am I doing things that take me ages?
Like flicking through the Yellow Pages!

I'll try vegging out and tuning in...
I really must empty that bin!

Suddenly!... I find myself just sitting...
Well, while I'm here I'll do some knitting.

I'll write a piece about how much I care...
But I really need to wash my hair.

It's no good, the words won't flow, and I can't settle...
Oh well... I'll just put on the kettle (Again!)
And have a fag...
Where did I put my bag?

I've been abandoned by my Muse!

So I'll go off and clean my shoes...
And watch the early evening news.

But wait... Here it comes... A witty line...
Oh really!... Is it dinner time?

It's just gone six...
Now where's the phone?
I'll call me mate and have a moan.

"No... I've not got time to go out to a club...
But I'll meet you for a quick one...
In the pub."

But write a poem for The Slam?
Well I really don't think I can...

...I've got far too much to do...

Diane Knowles

PANIC

Oh what made me say
that I'd do this today
My legs are a-quiver
Did you sense that last shiver

My heart's missed a beat
yes again I'll repeat
My heart's missed a beat
Can't I quickly retreat

    So what's this about
    I hear you all shout

It's my first poetry slam
oh bother, oh damn
Why did I agree
Won't you please let me flee

    So this poem's now done
    I'll say bye
    I must ....

Stuart Butler (The Stroud Football Poets)

THE IDEOLOGY OF SLAM

Now don't get me wrong, I quite like Slams,
I think it's great that the spoken and written word
Can pack places to the rafters
With people listening intently -
And I suppose that all of us,
Despite any pretensions
To radicalism, think that too.
We probably place, for a variety
Of unexamined cultural assumptions,
A greater emphasis on language
As a medium of communication than upon any other form,
Even though most people don't.
So, in that sense, despite any pretensions to modernity,
We are, seemingly, anachronistic.
(Not that I think there is anything necessarily wrong
With anachronicity, per se,
I make a living out of History.)

But all this is just the prologue -
What is the ideology of The Poetry Slam?
In a Slam, Art imitates Life - it is a lottery,
A game of chance and power.
And, again, don't get me wrong,
I think Slams have a place -
But rather than just subscribe to fashion
And to the Zeitgeist,
Tonight I'd like to challenge the assumptions
Underpinning Slam.
Despite the constant asseverations that Slams
Are not competitive,
Let's be honest, all other Slam life
Is quite to the contrary.

It is quintessentially judgmental
And, self-evidently, a knock-out,
Nature "red in tooth and claw"
And it is an exercise in Orwellian double-think
To claim otherwise.
Slams are essentially "Survival of the Fittest"
In the true sense of Darwin's original meaning,
Where "fittest" meant most appropriate;
And most appropriate to what?
Appropriate to the performer who has the most supporters
In the audience -
And this is no democratic model
Of equal voting and equal democratic rights,
It is one of unequal and unfair distribution of power.
And this model is hardly surprising
When we look and see where Slams come from -
America, the home of competitive self-help laissez-faire
Individualism,
Where you stand or fall, unsupported,
On your own two feet.
And, so you see, the reason I object to Slams
Is not the inanity of constant, but empty, rhyming couplets,
Nor is it the vapid superficiality of so much of the gender politics,
Nor is it the preoccupation with masturbation, swearing, shopping,
sex and cynicism;
No it's more that Slam professes to challenge Dominant Culture,
And, in fact, it merely confirms and replicates it.
Sometimes it has all the attractiveness of a slave auction,
Or a 19th century agricultural hiring fair,
So it's good to see the stage on the page;
It's time for a change.

Marcus Moore

WORDS PLOUGHED INTO SHARES

ἐν ἀρχῇ ἦν ὁ λόγος
in the beginning was the word
when every page was a slender leaf
and every song a bird

and every pen was a fountain
and every friend a pen
and stress was something rhythmical
and lays were something lyrical way back when

when in came the treasurers
the marketeers and bankers
to plunder the language
and keep the books the canker's

spreading and now everything has changed
into small change and rates of exchange
because money makes the world go round
there's even a poet called ezra pound

and we have income brackets
and a penny for our thoughts
and we're economical with the truth
because money talks

and when we open an account
it doesn't mean we start a tale
and we have to pay the piper
what is owed to a nightingale

and because speech is silver
we have to buy a loudspeaker
and when the poet coins a phrase
someone comes to read the metre

so just what are words worth
when silence is golden
if all the writers went on strike
would they be said to be holding

the country to ransom
i doubt it
but take away the WORD
and the WORLD is L without it

so invest in the alphabet
and speak and shout and sing
take an interest in vocabulary
before they cash it in

enrich your life with adjectives
and read and write and rage
line your pockets with imperatives
to hurl against the age

charge the city with accusatives
before we reach the stage
when a shareholder's certificate becomes
the bottom line on every page

Ralph Hoyte

ES IST NICHT MEINE AUFGABE

Today the machine for binding cartons of books with black tape broke down again but it wasn't my job to fix it. That's the job of the Italian underboss and he couldn't, so the experts were called in. They fixed it in a few minutes with a big hammer.

My job is to pack books: take books, stuff 'em in somehow, anyhow, pad with corrugated paper, shove onto the conveyor belt.

Outside the sun shines or doesn't, rain falls or doesn't, clouds float by or don't, traffic roars by or maybe it doesn't, people go about their business or maybe they don't - you can't tell in a hermetically sealed building and anyway, it's not my job. My job is to pack books.

Upstairs the secretaries secretarise, the computers compute, the bosses boss and watch their secretaries' legs and tight swinging bottoms, the directors direct and get their Mercedes washed by their underlings, the chairman chairmans, the accountants account, the building, hard concrete and concrete reflecting glass - oh, but I don't know, it's not my job. My job is to pack books.

In the busy city the street cleaners street clean, the taxi drivers taxi drive, the city councillors city council, the police police, the robbers rob, the Italians italianate and the Germans... germinate; the Federal Garden Show federal garden shows itself, the people people it and the ducks duck it, the children lick cones and the grown ups their mental lips, ice-cream drips onto hot, dirty fists...

... or maybe wind and rain, the smell of asphalt after a long period of sun and the hiss of rain-hit dust, the plonk of water into sodden soil where your boots sink in suddenly crossing the track for the small Bosch electric locomotive for the visitors which runs past pale mottled sycamores drearily lining tarmacadam ways - but I don't know, I don't know, damn it, it's not my job. My job is to pack books.

Maybe last night in the vastness of space the one-in-a-trillion-trillionth chance occurred again and a spark gulped itself into itself and erupted the fabric of being with yet another *'Let there be'* - and there was...

And maybe on some far off planet in some far off galaxy the mind-achingly beautiful form of some new Botticelli Venus rose through the clinging surf whilst all around the adoring shrimps waved their feathered feelers, *"Hail, Caesar, morituri te salutant"* -

- maybe

- or maybe not

I don't know, it's not my job:

My job is to pack books: take books, stuff 'em in somehow, anyhow, pad with corrugated paper, shove onto the conveyor belt.

Yet maybe among the flush of pink scalloped clouds the fair sea nymph still rises, Clairol-rinse endless streaming locks behind her, sea-waved wave-looped silver-bubbled belly, languidly gliding from the iridescent depths of the Hawaiian pineapple sea -

- only the distant spew of smoke, only the stinking oil patch, only the bobbing plastic bottle, only the grey spongy bodies of drowned boat people, only the - my job is to pack books, damn it.

Daniel Cassiel

RENEWING MY VISITOR'S PASSPORT

Twelve months in Fantasy City,
In a shirt so creased no iron can save it -

Licking white wine from red nipples
And never getting a headache,

Dreaming futures for the human race.

Fantasy City -

Where the person you stop in the street
Really is who you thought it was,
Where taxes go the other way.

Fantasy City.

It's
The thing.

I want to build my own house in the country,

Right after I finish building my own country
In the house.

Rosemary Gamsa
MAL'S MUSHROOMS

Casual invite
Sunday evening round at your place
    Tea for two
I come and smalltalk furniture and rent it's
    'Cosy'   while you pour
Two mugs of tepid cloudy brew
    Later
The room breathes life
            And shudders
Papered wall flowers dance and spin
Dotsido
In rhythm to the waves of carpet pile
The tide has turned
Against our feet
So   *let the games begin!*
Slow motion
Freezeframe hide and seek
You're animation as you cross the gap
From here
         To there
I miss the links as we come up
    Step
        By step
Swimming treacle paisley on the stair
I skip along the hallway
Featherlight graceful swan
Then flex my fingers lightspeed
    Blink
          The kitchen's gone
We lie   high
Above the crisscross battlefield
Head to head

Stalemate chasing dodging pawns
You're marooned on Cushion Island
And I drift raft-lazy on your bed
The world has stretched
     Elastic   shimmered   wonderful
Words
Exotic insects slip our grasp
I feel creation breathing   I'm a child
In love   I want to touch it all
Until at last
The board lies still
As stone
Pick the pieces up
               Formal
            Lost
                Cycle home

Peter de Meteor

BACK TO GODHEAD

Hare Krishna, Hare Rama
I dance down Oxford Street in my pyjamas
I'll give you a book or a record as a gift
But if you don't give me a £5 donation for it
I'll get pretty miffed

We're like a Hindu equivalent of the Salvation Army
We wear a different uniform
But we're just as bloody barmy!

Peter de Meteor

OPEN AIR SHAKESPEARE

I went to the zoo
To see 'The Taming of the Shrew'
The other animals were there too
But they were hidden from view.

Andy

LISA

My Dearest Darling Lisa
I will do anything to please ya
I will never make you blue
If you have the flu
I will always be with you

I love you

Andy

THE BRAVE
(the value of people)

You won't find them at a rave.

They're on the street
Helping people
Back on their feet.

You won't find them
On the golf course.
You won't find them
In the police force.

The Brave

They're in the hostels
For the homeless.

The Brave

They're priceless.

Charlotte Nile

SQUAT ON SUSSEX PLACE '95

Hopeful blue sky.
Empty dead house.
I'd expected banners and bustle
as part of the new 'Criminal In-Justice' centre.

But no-one around.

We bumped into Snake, whom Sophie knew:
"He's squatting here."
"Are you coming in?" he asks, seeing her.
"We've come to help sort things out," she said.
"Well I've got the key, follow me."

We walked in through stone dust
and darkness in the air.
Waiting for the others, who never came, we sat and talked
as Snake tried to get a fire going with chunks of the floor.
The first crackle became a vision of life:
with bright paint, meetings and triumphant protests.

Snake asked us question after question.
Hearing our silence he said:
"Sorry, I'm not interrogating you, I'm just lonely."
I noticed the blue sky and green branches
poking through the pane-less window.
       As if they didn't care.
The fire starting well, Snake nipped out for supplies.
We left, leaving him to an empty house and a fire which flickered and died?

Rupert Hopkins
MAYBE

Maybe it's all in
my imagination
that sense of total isolation
a room full of people
with whom
I constantly
fail to connect

Maybe it's all in
my imagination
the loneliness
the desolation
that passes through
my outstretched
electric finger tips

Maybe it's all in
my imagination
the voice that
cries out to me
but rushes past
hardly giving me
a second glance

Maybe it's all in
my imagination
that I should paint
put on a brave face
keep a starched
stiff upper lip
masquerade
hide my sense of
utter abandonment

stranded on that
invisible
spider webbed
rock face
abseil into
oblivion
turn the other
biblical cheek
expose it to the
harsh iced
driving rain
dull that out-pouring
of snow tear dropped
inner pain

Andrew Nash
PARALLEL LINES

We are not parallel lines.
Your eyes that deny so much
cannot disguise the truth
in the touch of your hands.

We are not parallel lines
but a simulation of
theoretical
mathematical
geometrical
phenomena.

Like the flip side of railway lines
into the horizon
we appear to be travelling
along side one another
never touching
when in truth we are slowly moving   further   apart.

Sara-Jane Arbury

FISH TALE

You pick me up off the floor.
With difficulty.
I am slippery and wet
With tears and sweat -
You need to use both hands.
No. It's not. Is it?
Not as easy as you thought it would be.
Best do it quickly.

Holding me in your arms
You lug me across the room
And slap me onto the kitchen table.
My one blank eye stares up at you
Mouth opening, aghast
As you take a knife
Sharp as a tongue
And split me from neck to navel.
Then
Reaching into
The warm mystery
Of my body
With scientific fingers
You rip and pull and tear and rupture
The delicate viscera
The intricate structure
Of my life and soul
Your saltwater splashes
Burn me red raw...

And when you feel there's nothing more
You wipe your hands and walk out of the door

Leaving me

Lying there

Gutted.

The Cutter
IT DOESN'T HURT ANYMORE

It doesn't hurt anymore
the back chat, the deceit
and all the ends that don't quite meet
the stupid rumours, all the lies
the bitter scorn behind your eyes
I've picked myself up off the floor
and I've got one foot through the door
and it really doesn't hurt anymore

And I don't think anymore
about the cost
the things I've lost
the scoffing and the sneers
the laughter ringing in my ears
the mindless fighting and the tears
the wasted months and wasted years
you know, it really doesn't hurt anymore

It doesn't hurt anymore
so let it rain, let it pour
you've lost the key, I've locked the door
and it really doesn't hurt anymore

Gill Higgins

FORGIVEN – REVISITED

I found a little toyboy
I think Alex was his name...
And I called him "Complete fuck-wit"
And he answered just the same...

I locked him in the bedroom, and I kept him there all night...

And Polly let my toyboy out...
Yes, Polly let my toyboy out...
She went and let my toyboy out...
And my toyboy ran away!

She said she didn't mean it
And I never said she did...
She said she needed skins and stuff,
And she knew where they were hid!

She said that she was sorry...
But it's difficult to catch,
A pretty-looking fast boy...
When you're looking for some hash!

She said that she was sorry,
And I really mustn't mind...
As there's lots and lots of toyboys
Which she's certain we can find!

If we look about the town,
In the pubs where toyboy's hid...
Then we'll put him in a big strong box
And write 'Toyboy' on the lid!

So we went to all the places...
Well the ones that sold strong beer!
And we made the sort of noises,
That toyboys like to hear...

I saw a kind of something...
And I gave a sort of shout...
"Look, that under-30's club,
It's my toyboy coming out!"

It was!... My toyboy
I'm as certain as can be...
And he had a sort of look,
"Oh shit she's recognised me!..."

And he had a sort of look...
As though he really ought to say,
"I'm really really sorry,
I didn't mean to run away!"

And Polly's very sorry too,
For-you-know-what-she-did...
But now she's got a crate for me
With 'Toyboy' on the lid!

So Pol and me are friends now...
'Cos it's difficult to catch...
A pretty-looking fast boy...
When you're looking for some hash!

Toby Farrow

EUROBOY

Bonjour Messieurs et Femmidoms
Je m'appelle Pierre.
I am a foreign exchange student
in Bournemouth beach seaside town.
I like English culture,
very nice,
I stick in naturally
like a sore thumb I think.

I savour many flavours of flesh
I like siliconesque, rumpmatic, nebulous babies, ah oui, oui!
I love you all!
I, how you say?
Bat all around the field
playing both sides of my handicap.
My bread
is buttered
on all four corners
& lands in the air, oui?

You know what I say you think.

But it is funny.
In English the girls lick my accent.
I say to girl in club
"Le ballon d'Alain est dans le salon."
It gets her very saxophone,
I tack her to my boudoir,
turn her into plywood
with drink alcoholic,
put on music sexy
& throw her up on the bed!

But in France I have to pretend
to be English to pull Les Filles,
c'est ne jolie pas!
I say "Your hair is like a bad collection of twigs
& your eyes are like chipped marbles,
I want to spit you to the ground
& shake you
until you run away
never wanting more!"

It seems to me,
why do I have to put on
an act to get the girls?
But that is the nature of sexiness, no?
Always chasing draylon
that will never come clean.

Emel

CINDERELLA'S SLIPPER

I know this man with a golden bouffant
and even his beard is quite bouffant
What is the meaning of this golden bouffant
groomed to perfection with intertwining complexities
like a shredded wheat biscuit, this golden bouffant?
His name, is Anton.

Dreaming in his workshop, a mere cobbler's son
"You have to carry the family business when I'm gone"
but all Anton could think about was his golden bouffant
A frustrated artist, because it was never perfected
Walking down the street, half proud when it was erected
Until one day
he met a toupée
named
Eduardos Carlos Discos Santos Sergio Mendez Salalamitos Casinos
who said he would make him famous throughout the land
from New York, Paris, London and Milan
Until
Eduardos Carlos Discos Santos Sergio Mendez Salalamitos Casinos
got so jealous
that he challenged him to a fight
which lasted a thousand days and a thousand nights
But Anton's bouffant was just too tall, muscley and strong
It came crashing down on
Eduardos Carlos Discos Santos Sergio Mendez Salalamitos Casinos
killing him instantly.

Now Anton is back working as a cobbler's son
and his bouffant is doing five years for manslaughter.

Tony Lewis-Jones

SAM REWRITES CASABLANCA

"Forget Paris, Rick" I said
"And forget that song.
You'll only start getting moody,
sink seven or eight bourbons,
then do your stupid impression of Hitler
invading Poland. It worries the clientele.
It isn't funny
when you finally fall off your chair, singing
the unofficial version of
'Deutschland Uber Alles'
and end up with your face on somebody's files.

"The girl's no good, I'm telling you.
I heard she had an affair
with Mussolini. Or maybe it was Rossellini.
Don't look at me like that.
If you had any sense about anything
you wouldn't be wearing a white tuxedo.
It shows the dirt
and this is a dirty town.
And as for women... Listen,
you're not the first to be charmed
by her taste in hats
and Scandinavian accent.

"You hear me?
Forget Paris, Rick
and forget that song.
Find someone younger.
Someone who knows how to whistle."

Mike Leeman

THE BEST AND WORST OF SCENARIOS

For Christmas
I received
(With some mild surprise)
Chocolate Body Paint.
"For sexy, velvety fun
With your partner."
Amusingly
(To me)
Attached to the side
Was a brush
Of almost
Wire wool standards.
Brillo themselves
Would be pleased
With its abrasive cleaning powers.

Three days
(Or rather nights)
Later,
In the cold,
Calculating time
Between
Festive cheer
And
Welcoming the new year
We
(My partner and I, not we as a collective whole)
Decided to try
The bottled saccharin sex.
I was to be the canvas
To her Carravagian strokes.

Creating a living masterpiece
Which people could see
Touch, taste, feel, smell,
And (hopefully)
Experience.

We tried the brush.
Yet after
A bleeding nipple
And scarred inner thighs
I suggested
(Or rather threw out of the window)
The thistled bristled devil,
And settled for a plastic butter knife.

The next few hours
Imaginations ran wild.
I was
Abstract man,
Renaissance man (though not the crap film with Danny DeVito),
Cubist man,
Man Avant Garde of the,
Naturalist man,
Not to mention very fucking happy.

The morning though held its own
Distant,
Grey eyed charm.
The bedside clock spoke of lateness for work,
So I flew out of bed
To grab my suit and tie
Or rather I tried.

Stuck to the bed
By molten love

I could not move
Legs,
Arms,
And bare backside
All plastered
To the silky,
Darkened layers
Of
Smoothest,
Creamy bedsheets.

I shouted for her,
Yet no reply came.
The lock-jaw
That is inevitable after a night of passion with Nutella
Had taken effect.
And her jelly-babied stomach
Weighed her down,
Pinning her sticky remains
To the remaining sticky bedsheets.

All we could do
Was lie there and laugh.
An odd sound from her,
More a guttural "Floob"
That sprayed glucose juices
From a frothing mouth.
This is,
Of course,
All my meanderings
And desperate attempts
At evil,
Sexual ideas for poetry.

We did actually try the above

Yet
Thanks to the extra added E-Numbers
And modified starch
(As well as my stray, blue, belly button fluff)
She took one lick
And was sick
On my stomach.

I had to have a cold shower.

christopher brooke

rash behaviour

my shaven cock and balls
snuffle around my bald thighs
like a baby anteater,
the in-growing pubic hairs
twist under raised and red skin,
nipping like blood ants

"c'mon, it'll be *fun*." she'd said

it took half-an-hour with the lady-shave,
quicker if we'd not drunk
all the wine, all the beer (*not at all*
if we'd been sober - this i know)

"lookit it!" she squealed, lifting it
like a dislocated finger:

we had the rudest sex
we'd had since we broke up.

yesterday, we ran into each other
both tried to remain serious:

"ooh, i feel like i've been got at
with a pine cone." she said

"mmmmm," i replied, scratching.

later, i met with a young lady
who, frustrated at my lack of interest,
complained

"what the hell is wrong with you?
can't you stay still?"

quickly, i changed the subject,
asked about the new painting
she was working on,
blissfully unaware of the stain
seeping through the crotch of my
beige slacks from the aloe
gel i'd administered
in a toilet cubicle
10 minutes previous.

Henry Lawrence
TIT BUM WILLIE

    D
tit bum willie bum tit bum willie bum
    D
tit bum willie bum yabba dabba doobah
    D
tit bum willie bum tit bum willie bum
    D
tit bum willie bum yabba dabba doobah

   D
Knickers, knockers, knackers
   D
crumpet, talent, lunch
   D
bollocks, buttocks, bristles
Am   *C*   *G*   *D*
waddo I could give her one

    Chorus

Jack the lad, part time swordsman
Wham, bam, thank you ma'am
drives a feller to distraction
punish Percy in the palm

    Chorus

Ugh I think that it's revolting
Ugh I think it should be banned
like running out of toilet paper
and you have to use your hand

    Chorus

CIDER

Clean cut,
I'm well slick, fucked - Full on loudmouth,
Gravelled guffaw at the promise of more,
Cider, stimulates my senses,
Scorcher, rip-roarer, it tickles, uh-huh, a-huh,
Splinters and shatters,
And every atom sings in blissful monotone.
Cider blows my brains apart, vertical - horizon,
Last time I had cider I was sick on a goat.
I drink it coz it's cheap like, an' it gets I drunk.
White Lightning whips my ass,
Spectra slices sound,
Blackthorn B.P.M. - leads the apple anthem,
Definitely a dry blackthorn day,
And I learnt all that from one sip,
Now I'm going to down another
- So it can make you creative?
'Course it can - In excess you dress to impress with a bit more flair,
Open wide the shutters, smashed, hammered, plastered, spannered,
Soluble fizz, apple jizz, South-West wrecked on cider whizz,
Let it stimulate up your world.
A different space, I'm just going through a cider phaze,
Kingston Black 5 gallon - Bang on!
Cheddar Valley whettens the palate,
Reality flattens then keels sideways
Warped to the extent of hangover-head,
You want to move but you can't be bothered,
You mumble mix-mashed utters,
You want some more?
You know you can take it,
Ride on it, crest of a wave,
Cider sensation
Peak of imagination

Scrumpy jump-start, gassed sweet bubbly,
Psychedelic lovely-jubbly, tastebud-killer, stomach-filler,
Nothing cures a hangover like 18 bottles of Spectra,
Ashton Vale, murky, berserky, shirty, flirty,
After K - collectable special edition, it's easier to make the right decision,
Copperhead fucks me head sweetly, almost any type can keep me on one,
Slurred strong, shifted, shaft on, fast on, funk on, punk on, drink on cider
An' all your dreams come true, so on yer bike, down the offie
Coz we jus' ran out,
Ooooh - Aaaah.

Pete Brown

A BIT OF ROUGH

Now, I'm neither a tit - or a leg man
though I admit - to liking small, tight arses
But what really turns me on - is the accents
   of the middle classes
Whenever I hear the round vowels
   of a good, or convent school
I feel a twitch, my legs go weak, I sometimes even drool
   Cos I'm a fool
for constant consonants and precise pronunciation
   I'm made up wiv - a sibilant fricative
I'm such a sucker - for a classic education
   It's a strange taste - I acknowledge
for a boy who ran from Wandsworth High
   to wanna run thru - Cheltenham Ladies College
But that's just me - I've always been a contrary sorta guy
I just follow my impulses - I dunno why
I know I'd prob'ly feel more at home - wiv a Tracy or a Sharron
Stand more chance of getting a bone - wiv a Carol or a Karen
But I'm not interested - I don't wanna Donna - it's a dilemma
I want girls called Charlotte or Pippa
   I want an Honour or an Emma - and it's always bin the same
It's like designer labels - I like pretentious names
   But, Hey - I'm just a man at C&A
   I can't afford Pringle or Jaeger
I was born to a world of Marks and Sparks
(I'm not knocking their knickers - I just prefer Janet Reger, OK)
I don't think I'm be'en out of order - I think you can 'ave any girl you want
as long as you can afford 'er - For surely, this class thing's all just tosh
You can even 'ave a Princess these days - if you've got enough dosh
   Or so they say
Which is where this second, socially divisive barrier - gets in my way
I work too 'ard for my living - to earn a rich man's pay
   which is why I'm feeling harassed
I'm not just socially - but I'm financially embarrassed

I can't keep up wiv those city types - or them financial fellers
Which is why I'm always cast to play - the uncouth part of Mellors
Which is the 'ard part - while I've got a soft heart
    and want to be loved for myself
Not for my hint of danger - my air of lowlife -
And despite my lack of wealth
    to be a toy - is not enough
    I don't wanna be forever - just a bit of rough
A rich girl's plaything - someone's bit of stuff
Cos I'm a real person - in my own right
    and no-one's bit of fluff
    Cos I've got feelings –
and I'll admit now - to all here present
that the reason I keep trying to bed these debs
    is that - I've always felt like an aristocrat
    Trapped - in the body of a peasant

Rachel Bentham
JUST A FEELING

I've been told
that I'm an intelligent woman -
it was meant to be a compliment.
I've been told that I'm an intelligent woman
by men who can't help looking
at my mouth, my breasts, my legs -
and while they're telling me
I'm an intelligent woman
I feel like they're thinking more
about what's in my pants
in relation to what's in their pants;
but that's just what I feel
and there's no real evidence...
Except the million billion images
of women as mouths, as breasts, as legs,
as anything but simply intelligent -
and, after all, feelings
are such flimsy, feminine things
I know there's not much room for them.

John Kandinsky

GETTING IT RIGHT
(written for St.Valentine's Day)

They climbed the stairs together, him and her.
Climbed in the loveliness of their passion,
leaving their guests to nudge and wink
and remember their own time.
Their own long-ago weddings.

Both started to undress.
He, with his shirt and coat over a chair
just as mother had taught,
and she, coyly removing each item
like small gifts for him to savour.

He picked up the discarded trousers,
smiled and said
"put these on."

She, thinking this some game, obliged.

The smile left his face
and he pointed the finger.

"Remember" says he
"this is the last time
you'll wear the trousers here."

She silently removed the trousers,
placing them compliantly
over the chair at the side of the bed.

Picking up the small,
triangular transparency
of her own discarded linen
she says "Put these on."

He, taking the flimsy garment
no bigger than a tissue,
looked in wonderment.
"I couldn't get into these" he says.

"No" says she,
"and if you don't change,
you never will."

Avril Staple

THE APPLE POEM

Biting into the green skin
sucking the juice from the white flesh
mashing it between her molars
to release the flavour from the pulp.

Eve, the naked virgin is
tasting fruit for the first time
and suddenly she knows.

She looks at Adam's unhealthy skin and says
"Go on, taste it. Taste the knowledge."
"Wot, an' waste a good night's drinking?"
"Yeah. Reach out to the world beyond the sofa
and see the truth of all human kind."
*"Football's on. Go an' make a cuppa or
something."*

Through the eyes of her new wisdom
she sees the washing, covers it
and thinks "fuck it."
At night she dances under the moon
eating apple after apple that
falls from the tree of life
filling herself with Golden Delicious wonder.

And next morn fresh and alive
with the sweetness still lingering on her tongue
she says again, begs
"Bite it. Taste it. Be like me.
Unchain yourself from narrow vision
and see the world beyond
chips and beans to the afters."
"Where's my black jumper?"

190

With determination she gathers
a variety of apples,
Cox's, Spartans, Ida Reds,
Granny Smiths
She lays them out in front of him
She strokes their smooth perfect roundness
Her lips close around each one
her eyes focused on his
She tells him
how the juice caresses her taste buds
how exciting the first bite is
how her body is suddenly filled
with a rich source of vitamins and minerals.
"Suck it. Suck the juice. Allow the flavour
to arrange your senses."
And Adam says

*"The thing about tinned peaches is
they're sterile. Apples give me the shits."*

She was the one who changed.
It was her that unleashed the
richness of variety in the diet.
It all started with
One Apple
One Bite
One Desire.

And it took guts.

Rosemary Dun

THE OTHER SIDE - A FOOTBALL RANT

Have I missed the point of Football's appeal?
The love and belonging I can see is real
An excuse, if you like, to kiss and to hug
To wear scarves and sport banners, belong to a club.
And the sport is exciting
The drama, the spills, writ large on our screens
Full of passion and thrills.
I can see this side as benign, life affirming,
It's the aggression I find pretty scary.

For me it displays what I hate about the Right
With its blind allegiance to the Monarchy,
A determination to fight
On the pitch and on the terrace that's tribal, nationalistic,
With Union Jack-the-lads looking hard and sadistic
Masculinity gone mad, enough testosterone to sink us
It's the expression of aggression, I don't get.

Then there are those who maintain that Football's High Art
When most quite frankly couldn't give a fart for all that bollocks.
Instead, Football commentary is the place
Where banality has a grace and favours home.
Where many clichés, not a few,
Are bandied by sports commentators - players too.
Is this ironic, post-modernist, or plain tosh?
Is there a school where sporting superlatives are taught?
Or is this Football language thought to be authentic working class?
Seems condescending to me.
And I really cannot see why these people
Aren't told they would be toss pots
Anywhere else.

Or do I miss the point here too?
And it's a mark of a sportsman true
To proudly speak as if education was for wimps
And they had something better - ie. Football - to do at school.
This is another rant of mine
Why can't language and Football combine?
Stroud Football Poets do it with aplomb!
But as I remember Cantona
Was treated as coming from somewhere out past Mars
Cos he's French and poems are for poofters.

And yet... I remember Football Scores
On Grandstand, on Saturdays, sometime after Four
When we'd close our eyes and try hard to guess
The results by the tone of the announcer's voice.
Win, Lose or Draw, Dad would sit in his chair
Checking his Littlewoods coupon
And we'd have to shut up, couldn't talk, wouldn't dare,
Or we'd watch as he became an indoor Footballer from his chair.
He'd twitch and he'd groan, legs going, kicking and weaving
As he followed the game, attention never leaving
The action on the box.
And how he'd leap from his seat, let out a huge cheer
If his side seemed anywhere near scoring a goal.
Or he'd jump, shout: "Offside!"
"Come on Ref, are you blind!"
And I'd watch amazed and happy at my Football Dad
Be proud, try to comment when he'd turn to me and say -
"Did you see that? What's he doing? That's a free kick Ref!"
It really made my day
To see Dad - that distant figure
Transmogrify into Dad of big emotions
It was awesome and beautiful to see,
And I'd hold my breath, and make a wish,
A wish that he'd have some left over,
Please, for me.

Now Dad sneers, says players are soft
And that in his day they bloody well wouldn't want to hug and to snog.
It's a different generation.

And I'm not sure if it does say anything about the Nation
When huge emotion on the pitch spills over into aggravation
In the crowd.
Or is it the other way round?
And what is that saying out loud about us?
Is it defusing, or using, or is it abusing?
A necessary reality? A mass display of nationality?
An expression of masculinity on the macho side?
A tribe? All of these and more?

In my life Football's been on my margins,
A male sub-culture, with an alien message
But maybe I should look closer
Maybe it holds one of the keys
To us.
Or did I miss the point yet again and that really
It's Just A Game?

Adam Horovitz

OVERHEARD IN A LONDON PUB

I'll tell you what I want.
Yeah, I'll tell you what I want.
I'll tell you what I fucking well want.

I want a pint of that fucking piss-weak   fucking expensive   fucking fuck of an
excuse   for what you say **passes** for beer in this fucked up pub.   And I want it
now and I ain't going to fucking pay for it. No.   Fuck off, I'm kidding,   just give
me the beer.

I'll tell you what I want.
Yeah, I'll tell you what I want.
What I fucking well want.

I want you to stop behaving like a jackass jack-in-the-box   jumping up and down
with that fucking inane grin on your fucked up face   trying to fucking well cheer
me up.   **I don't need no fucking platitudes.**   I could take this fucking bar
stool and shove it so far up you'd be fucking grinning wood for a week.

I'll tell you what I want,
yeah, I'll tell you what I want.
I'll tell you what I motherfucking want.

I want more money than you'll ever have,   enough to fucking buy you, buy
your poxy fucking house,   your soul - fucking everything.   Enough to turn your
fucking heart to blisters. Enough to wear a full fucking metal jacket and blow the shit
out of the fucking dross that swarms about me   all the fucking time. Pistols,
shotguns, fucking AK47s. Fucking yeah.   Fuck Uzi's.   Fuck this shit.
Fuck it all.   I'll bury the fucking lot...

I'll tell you what I feel.
Yeah, I'll tell you what I feel.
I'll tell you what I motherfucking feel.

I feel nothing except the slow burn of my girlfriend's hand on some other fucker's dick.

Alison Brumfitt

ON BAD LANGUAGE IN PERFORMANCE POETRY

There's a lot of bad language in performance poetry,
I think it's fucking unnecessary.

People should learn to enunciate their expletives.

Lawrence Pettener

THE GATHERING

The storm's all in the gathering.
An air of magic, trees create.
The wind, it kicks your head in.

All afternoon and all evening
horny and wired you wait.
The storm's all in the gathering.

You'll walk out, done with waiting
the storm to penetrate.
The wind, it kicks your head in.

It rumbles faintly, without lightening.
Winter's wine is in the crate.
The storm's all in the gathering.

Tonight it takes while only giving
an oppressive, heady weight.
The wind, it kicks your head in.

It dwindles off to nothing
this all, which once was great.
The storm's all in the gathering.
The wind, it kicks your head in.

John Kelly

SOUTH

Riveted,
Riven in cold steel,
Shot bolted in iron,
Ten hours salt sweating
To flesh the skeleton hull
For a pound or two
In my pocket
Like my 'da and gran'da before.

The links of this chain
Will be broken,
And I shall the breaker be.
The beer swilling swagger
On Saturday night
Has lost its appeal for me
And the echoes of old songs
In the tenement close
Have no magic or mystery

I'm neither green nor orange,
Friend or foe
The drum beating and bugle blowing
Of the bowler-headed boys
Leaves me cold,
And the Corpus Christi processions
Are no better

If these hands
That have tempered sheet metal
And bent the iron brow
Cannot be shown new ways,
Then I may as well
Play the last card now

With my last week's wages
I will buy a suit
From the ten pound tailor
And trade the gramophone
For a silver cigarette case
Stamped with my name

And on Monday Morning
I shall take the first train . . . .
. . . . South

Ray Gange

THE POSTMAN COMETH

Now comes
the postman
pushing
his cart full
of mysteries and
mundanity
which one
will it be?
What do I Get?
No sleep at night
that's
for sure and
whatever it is
will it be
what it is
Or
another metaphor
everything seems to be
a metaphor
what was 1984
a metaphor
for?
How about some
straight talking
not some
post modernist
post feminist
post this and that
around the houses
bullshit.
Give it to me
straight.

I don't need
a chaser
to go with it
just
gimme some truth
you know I
can
take it
Go on, try me.
I don't mind if you
ream my arse
but don't tell me
it's true love
when it's just your
metaphor for
male supremacy within
a socio-feminist debate
Hey wait a second
how did we get
back on that groove?
Put it back
in an envelope with
return to sender
on it
cause I don't
want it
and I don't
need it
so don't con me
into taking it

Gerry King

THE CAR CLEANER

My arms are hard and sinewy I clean cars.
Passionately.
Put your body in my hands,
Let me soap and caress every line and curve.
You could stay inside and watch me.
I like to see my reflection in my handiwork.
It justifies my whole existence.
Rather like buying the largest items on offer in the supermarket.
Hauling them heavily home.
I feel I've shopped well.
Nothing worth possessing comes easy.

I see the water pearling off the panelling.
I chamois shine quick time to avoid streaks.
I clean in a sequence, an order.
Each vehicle mapped out for invasion.
Starting with the roof and moving on,
I sweat silently inside my Velcro-sealed suit.
I deftly deal with the bonnet and boot.
Doors in the shade and sunny side,
Don't interrupt with a roof rack.
When I lose myself I just seem to glide.

The thoughts, my dreams have a special place,
Each day more precious, I have to protect them,
Like my hands... yet I never wear gloves.

Rosalyn Chissick

STALKER

He pins butterflies
to the cork-tiled walls
of his room,
likes the way
their colours never fade.

He follows her
for weeks, the way
she walks the streets
like a promise.

He calls her
at odd hours
to hear her fear
shiver along his back.

He stands on her driveway
at night,
scuffs his toes
on the crazy paving.

He watches her shape
ripple behind the curtains.
Inside his head
he roams
as if her rooms
have no doors.

PVT *West*

ARACHNE

This is my time of year, dear.
My territory stretches from here to well, to right over   there
I am in your way? So be it, dear.
I have a web site daily to repair
& I am waiting in for prey.
I don't apologise - to humans or to flies.
Just let one wing-tip but brush one spot
On any hardened filament of extreme tenuity
(the outpourings of my inner reservoir of creativity)
Or any of my sticky dots strategically
                              placed by me like barbs on wire
Kiss & I'll not miss. With my venom and my enzymes
I will sting inject & suck with my chelicerae.
Also, I am about to mate.
Where is he? Oh, somewhere near, dear,
I am sure. No doubt depositing his sperm
Online in a tangled web, practising charm.
Excuse my togs but I am arthropod, oviparous
As a bird (but more proliferous)
& I do not sing or sit but cocoon my sprogs
In silk (I let them self-incubate). Yes, my mate -
Their future father - & I - are geeing-up our genitalia.
Before he comes over to this incandescently-spun paraphernalia
Of mine to flirt
                    he will gloop up his goo into his pedipalp
In order to squirt
                    it all into my epigyne.
All I have to do is hang around here and wait.
He's not likely to be unique. His physique
In comparison to mine, to be frank, will be pathetique
but afterwards I might invite him to dine.
My main course? Of course he'll be mine.

I'll unfold my pernicious fangs, like so - Oh, don't go -
You're not jealous are you? That I have man on the menu?
I may be upside down but with ten simple eyes I can recognise
The Scorpio in you - we're family! We are not unalike, you & I
We both contain unfertilised eggs
Both have hairy legs, both want nooky
This is our time of year, dear - our time to get lucky...
Can't we be friends? You must allow
This is an impressive web that bars your way.
Ten days & I'll be fucked, fed and off - OK?
Promise I'll only leave behind a floating filament to show.

If you barge through, though, I warn you, I can tamper.
At night can scamper up your spine into your skull at will,
Squeeze your brain, spin an arachnoid membrane tight
& before you wake with headaches and with fright
In nightmare after nightmare you will dream of me - Arachne...
This is my time of year, dear...

Flo Kirk

LADY KILLER

Lady killer... a lady who kills
And thrills
At the thought of murder most horrible
Horrific   Terrific   **Orgasmic**

You see it takes talent to kill
It takes talons to kill
It takes guts and gauze and lace to kill.
I'm a ladykiller
A man eater
Stalking silent streets in skin-tight silk
Or vanishing in voluptuous velvet and veils
I never fail.
Luring luckless lads to my pain-filled pad
I'm a black widow... Aphrodite with a death-like bent
Dropping demons with my dagger-filled glare
Serpents stop and stutter with my stony stare
I'm a dream devil
A nightmare nymph
What are your chances if you buy me a drink?
They say "she'll change for the love of a good man"
Yeh right. Save your breath...
...you haven't got too many left.
I'm death on legs...
...even if they are rather pretty ones.
Infinite change in infinite variety
I get bored with murder accepted by society.
I'll strut my stuff in seedy Soho...
...You live for whips and chains?...
...That's good!! I always said "live for whips and chains
Die by whips and chains."

Lorena Bobbett, she was my pupil
Failed the first test... should have diced it
Or sliced it, or even made hot dogs.
I gave up teaching when she fucked up
Poor John Bobbett didn't know his own luck.
Went back to doing what I love most
Cut out his eyes and watch them roast.
Passion-filled nights in my palace of pain
Don't make plans to live again.
I'm a vampiric valkrey searching for veins
An Amazon woman with no old flames.

So gentlemen please sleep well in your beds tonight
And pray that you wake to dawn's soft light.

Gary Cox

FROST BITE

As a child the summers seemed longer
The bright autumn days would greet the first frosts
And the chill of the night would be a sharp contrast to the warmth of the day

As a child I was fascinated by the frost
Mesmerised I would step out into the night
And allow myself to be enveloped by this wintry cloak
Relishing the nip I knew I could retreat to the sanctuary of my mother's
home
Before I was bitten

When we first met we enjoyed each other's heat as we made love in frozen
fields
Insatiable was our desire to fall together
Outside, far from all that troubled us
Relishing the nip we knew we could retreat to the sanctuary of our own
homes
Before we were bitten

It was my heart that became frozen
It was my desire to seek the warmth of another
It was me, it was me

She left me, she left her mind, she left a note and she left this world

Each night I feel the chill
Palpable, thick, heavy and oppressive
She has not forgotten, she has not forgiven

The temperature drops as she enters my room

I will never relish this nip
As I know I can't retreat any further than the sanctuary of this home

I Will Be Bitten

Elizabeth Cowley Guscott

REMEMBERING YOU

Cobwebs
　　tremble on the window pane
silken threads
　　glisten damp with dew.
Golden
　　lies one dandelion late
all that's left
　　to remember you.

A picture
　　in the window stands
two smiling faces
　　with arms entwined.
Sunshine
　　glitters on the frame
your face is sweet
　　your lips like wine.

The spider
　　waits for its prey
one wasp
　　did swerve, then flew on by.
I wish
　　that I had seen your web
no tears
　　now would cloud my eye.

Soon the cobwebs
　　all will be gone
September's dew
　　will turn to rain.
The leaves
　　are falling, all colour spent
Spring soon will come
　　I'll smile again.

Jean Hathaway

UNTITLED

You
> won't answer if I ring

or
> if you do

you'll
> be very brief
> hurt and hurtful.

Before I go to the phone
I put potatoes on to boil,
pale hostages to fortune.

Never did burned potatoes
taste so sweet.

Polly Carr
FAMILIAR

The warped wood gap above the letter box lets in a flap
Of light which lands slab sunny on the floor.
Seen through the hazy glass of the screen door
It looks familiar, nearly manilla, like a letter
And each time I go past I pause and think to pick it up
Before I remember it's a coax, a missive hoax
Not a letter, not a letter from a lover, not a flyer
Not a circular. Not a rejection from a job application
Not a charity supplication, a reminder to renew my subscription
Not a party invitation, not a bill
Not a poster for a jumble sale to be held in a dark church hall
Not a dear jane or a pamphlet from god
Not a mailshot or snapshot offers
Not a note from my neighbour
It looks so familiar
And each time I go past I pause and think to pick it up
To hold the sunlight shimmer
Before I remember, it's a postcard from summer.

Rudi Mould

A GRAND PIANO

Dedicated to Cuban pianist 'Rubén González' and bass player 'Cachao'
who have brought Cuban music into my life.

A grand piano,
tarnished from age in a Cuban home,
weary from woodworm gnawing at its soul,
yellow keys that once were white,
still glows from the dusting, the running
of its maestro's fingers
over the familiar terrain,
that conquered a day's strain.

Music -
boleros, cha cha chas, sones,
and the great descargas.
Still there after all those years,
sung to a glass of rum and ice,
sparkling prism reflecting smiles,
of a señorita hanging out,
sunshine singing,
familiar lines of dancing poetry,
juggled over the blacks and whites.

This piano has been taken over the hill,
carried through the streets,
wheeled into concert halls and
propped up on rickety floorboards.
Its maestro knows this all too well,
pulling up stools dressed in a suit, singing with his band;

"oyela, como suena la flauta,
listen up, how the flute rings.
Como mi ritmo, no hay dos,
like my rhythm, there aren't two."

Bury the times of 20's and 10's,
Big Dollar Bills,
fast talking gangsters buying up the cabarets.
The ladies so touchable,
the nights so loveable and long.
It goes on...

Today,
a grand piano stands decadent,
wood dust accumulated round its feet.
It's the final chance maestro,
lift up its lid, expose its soul,
play some more,
to tell a story of those days when
music flirted in the clubs,
and Havana's revolution
was danced by feet
that scraped cha cha chas throughout the nights.

Joseph McKillen
UNBALANCED SCALES

How vaguely the last few days have passed.
How little interest they held for me.

While out walking i heard
the conversations of birds
sweetly sung melodies
saying more than words.
Oh how
i could silence their talk
with the throw of a single stone.
Wherever my gaze fell
i saw hands joined with hands.
How
warm the loose change
inside my pockets felt.

Anger, self-pity
mere diversions for my inward thoughts
to keep them from uniting and
setting fire to my heart
and i
forced to endure the flames
with no escape.
With only time
to decide when the flames
have burnt enough.

i never saw her again.

A LA RECHERCHE DU TEMPS PERDU....

When I look at the Proust novel you gave to me, lying unread
I think of you and miss you.
When I hear our song on the radio I sigh and
I think of you.
When I walk upon the moor, our moor, with an empty cold hand
I think of you and miss you.
When I watch our film I cry alone and
I think of you and miss you.
When I gaze upon our daughter's face, sleeping in unknowing peace
I think of you and miss you.

One selfish driver who'd had one for each road
Why didn't he miss you ?
Why didn't he miss ?
Why didn't he ?
Why didn't ?
Why ?
Oh.... how I miss you......

Pat Jones

SMILE

If I should die and you remain,
Think of me now and again;
Not as a wingèd angel in a billowing gown but as me up above
Smiling down on you, those I love.
Hush my sweet child, do not sigh
For I shall be with you should you cry.

You will see me in a thousand things
Remember me when the robin sings
And as, with a rush, the years roll by
We shall be reunited, you and I.
So I say to you my family and friends,
Smile with me so love never ends.

Marty Godden

TOWER OF STRENGTH

YOU
are my Tower of Strength
someone to lean on in trouble
It is to You I come each time I hurt
when the problems surround me
from all angles and many depths
It is to You I come
to keep me alert

but please be there for me still
somehow I need You more now
So it is to You I look for good advice
the ghosts are crowding in on me
circling my mind with a fearful force
So it is to You I look
as You are wise

just be my friend now and forever
I look up to You and respect You so
Now it is towards You I run so fast
to keep me safe from the hurt and pain
and to save me from my doubting self
Now it is to You I surrender
at long last

YOU
are my
Tower of Strength

so

treat

me

gently

Sally Hearn

IRAN AID

I didn't ask your name,
I'm sorry.
I didn't ask from where you came -
I'm sorry.
You see,
I'm a selfish western bitch
too protected to contemplate
grief such as this.
I was de-sensitised
de-personalised
but right now I'm traumatised
by the pictures of your dead husband.
You're too close to home -
inside my lounge I can switch you off,
but not my door - I can't close it. . .
Please go -

No - stay - have tea
English style
not kind, not caring -
just domicile.

"John come quickly"
(He'll know what to say).
He's travelled her country,
knows the lie of her land.
He's seen horrid sights
outside TV land.
He'll write a cheque
and understand why
her husband was executed
by her government,
why she walks English streets
on this cold wet Advent.

She says her children are lost
her husband tortured and dead,
there's no room for Christmas
in the Islamic jihad.

Jasper Hardhat

LONDON TRIP 1-3

PART 2

The tube, nicotined windowed express
Tight-lipped eyes stare into space
Lost in a visage of black-looped destiny
When the stranger stands out
Seeing the life that runs flat
In the eyes of the discontented commuters
Their eyes all run flat
"Look, can't you see the wonders that surround?"
On and on he burbles, verbal assaulting
Whilst in their heads
"Why don't you shut up?"
You can see the fear in their eyes
Until the journey's almost complete
Yet the jester feels less
Than someone else's excess
Inside he's waiting for the excuse
To escape the hum-drum
Of yet another urban drama

Claire Berry
STRESS

Haven't got time to sleep
Too many things to do
People to see places to go
God I hate the weekend everything stops.
Can't get anything done
Moving house three appointments on Thursday
Holiday need rucksack stereo alarm clock most important
Need to sort my life out by tomorrow 5pm
Or the world might end!
Sweaty palms palpitations
Endless thoughts trail into each other
Shit forgot shit I'm late
Sorry can't stop to chat
Got to go!

HURRY WORRY HURRY WORRY

Sort out college courses yoga classes voluntary work
Write a poem for the damn slam
Need a job need some cash
So much to do so little time!!
Meet a friend have a coffee
Sorry can't stop only got 5 spare minutes
Can't even read my diary
Blue red black ink
Crossed scribbled dates reminders notes
Phone numbers...... shit wrote it on a bus ticket
Used it to dispose of my chewing gum!
Need change for the phone
Call DSS Housing Department National Express Bank College Library!

HURRY WORRY HURRY WORRY

So much to do so little time!!
I could die tomorrow get run over by a bus
Hope not haven't got time!

HURRY WORRY HURRY WORRY

Eat fast think fast get fast
Missed the bus - damn bus drivers again!
Lost my contact lens
Don't have time to look
Can't find specs to see
Stuffing some cling film in my eye
Shit I'm late again
Shit I forgot to call the DSS!

HURRY WORRY HURRY WORRY

Need a holiday
Haven't got time
Panic attack - only a quick one mind!

Slow down

Chill out

WHERE'S THE VALIUM? ! !

John Trolan

I DON'T LIKE FEELING LIKE THE WAY I DO

I don't like feeling like the way I do,
It's a mixture of resentment, rage and the colour blue.
If you're not sure what I'm on about, keep an ear tuned.
I'll explain each and every one of them before I'm through.

Resentment is a feeling that can strip me bare.
It can have me crawling up the walls and tearing out me hair.
It's usually caused by someone close, for whom I love and care,
Whom I'd give my very life for, but when I need them, they're not there.

Rage is caused by Tory canvassers who knock upon my door.
They patronise the homeless, the crippled and the poor.
When they ask "Who is to pay for these?" throwing their eyes up to the air,
I tell them "You, you rich bastard. Now piss off out of here."

The colour blue is something special brought on by little things,
Like when you sit to have a shit and the telephone rings!
You quickly wipe your arse and dash, to see what news it brings...
It stops, just as you get there, echoes off on little wings...

Now I don't like feeling like the way I do,
I'd like to feel happy... orange... you know, something new.
There again, if that means joining the blue crew,
Then bollocks to it, I'm alright feeling like the way I do.

Jamie Caddick

A TRAINSPOTTER'S LIFE FOR ME

Standing on the platform
At five-and-twenty-to,
I spot a locomotive
In a darker shade of blue.
The driver puts the brakes on,
It makes an awful din
And I can see the people watching,
Pointing, saying "Look at him!"
"He's a trainspotter!"
"Oh! How appalling!"
"He hasn't got a life."
In the distance you can hear a calling
"Spend more time with me" - that's my wife!
I admit I might look like a weirdo,
A moron, a goofball, a freak,
But I ask you now
What other past-time will allow
You to spot the InterCity every week?
To stare at its beautiful panelling,
Gaze in awe at its pistons and shafts,
With a wholemeal packed lunch
I don't ask for much
I don't want fancy parties and laughs.
My life is quite nice as it stands, thanks.
I truly don't need your advice.
Most people don't notice
My acute halitosis
My nose hair, ear wax or head lice.
Plus the raincoat you see that I'm wearing
Not dirty, it's brand spankin' new,
In this ensemble I don't feel like a womble,
Entire kit: Oxfam £9.82.

Of course, with the women I'm hopeless,
Trainspotting mars potential to pull.
I'm naturally quite shy
Though I did use to try
To be liked and shed the image of a fool.
But watching the trains is my hobby,
It excites, enthralls, fills me with passion,
Though I do feel the flak
Wearing my favourite anorak
It's never been in let alone out of fashion!
I'm married, you know, to my Edith,
My sweetheart, my diamond in the rough.
And when I first saw her
My reaction was "PHWOOOOEEERRRR!!"
I thought "Blimey! What a cracking bit of stuff!"
In her luminous green shell-suit bottoms
She was gorgeous, a sight to behold.
I'd drunk a whole half a shandy
So I was feeling quite randy,
I felt perky enough to be bold.
Well, before this I'd been chatting in "Trainspeak"
To a sprightly young filly called Jude.
At my mention of train-tankers
She said "God, you're a wanker!"
And stormed off - don't you think that was rude?
So, Edith and I got on nattering,
Our rapport was dynamic, we clicked.
I liked trains, she loved plants,
We both collected old stamps,
I guess you could say I was licked.
Three weeks later we marched up the aisle,
I was the happiest man in the land,
With my trains and my stamps
Plus a slight twinge of cramps
It was a dream I could never have planned.

Edith's in the larder at home now,
Knocking up a blancmange or a stew.
She doesn't get harassed
And I no longer feel embarrassed
To say "Spherical Shaft Pistons" - it's true!
I've my anorak, my pen and my notebook,
And though people may think I'm a bore,
I stand here at the station
And with great deliberation
Jot down numbers I've not seen before!
Six-Five-Special and Railtrack 120,
Scribble them down - quick! - I'm not that aloof,
And there is no debatin'
This is fascinatin'
Just watching me - isn't that proof?

Jeremy Dixon
HAVING WORDS

You can call me stupid
Call me fat
Say I've no discernment
'cos I like Take That
Adolescent, immature
Just going through the motions
Remote, reserved
Out of touch with my emotions
Forget my name
Call me Walter
Compare my chin
To the Rock of Gibraltar
A vicious drunkard
Playing out some scene
A dysfunctional dreamer
A bitter old queen
I hope it won't upset you
When I let you know the score
That you've just said nothing
I haven't heard before
Except
You may well die
In distress and great pain
If you ever dare call me
Pathetic
Again

E Woodsford

LES REGRETS

When I was just a young girl,
Had senses all a-whirl,
My long, lean, leathered lover
Loved her Harley more than me.

And so,
Sod off, I said.

And then,
She did.

And now,
She's dead.

And me?
I live at home,
With mother.

Ralph Hoyte

LILY

The little girl who lives in the
house had a rabbit but it
wouldn't behave it wouldn't
come to her indeed it ran away
whenever anyone came near as
rabbits do so she punished it for
not loving her she poked it with a
stick she took away its water and
gave it no food because you see
rabbits have to love little girls yes
rabbits have to love little I HATE
YOU I HOPE YOU HAVE A
HORRIBLE LIFE she screamed at
it I HOPE YOU GET RUNNED
OVER WITH A CAR I DON'T
WANT YOU so it was given to
the old people at a nearby
hospital who've got lots of love
left over which nobody wants the
little girl's got a Barbie Doll now

Louise Law
PMT

I slam the cups down on the table as angrily as I am able
to let him know that he's a jerk   reading the paper whilst I work
I don't need to act this way   slogging my guts out every day
the cooking roster's on the door   he knows how to scrub the floor

but that's not good enough for me
a downtrodden housewife I'd rather be

He's home from work   he says hello
He's worked all day   he's lost his glow
He greets me with   a weary smile
I grunt a greeting   after a while

He reaches out to give me a hug
I pick up the rubbish and straighten the rug
I busy myself with anything
to make it look like I'm suffering

He attempts to give my neck a rub
tries again to get a hug
Although his hands are feeling good
my sullen face is made of wood

I will not laugh I shall not grin
the venom is just inside my skin

I'll go to any lengths to be
the centre of disharmony
If thumping dishes he ignores
I'll storm around him slamming doors

Stirring up a family row
the kids have got entangled now
Despite the fact that it's absurd
I must have the final word

Satisfied I walk away
ready for another day
Life goes by without a hitch
this ain't PMT   I'm just   a bitch

Ali Chapman

I AM WHEREVER I AM

Purge yourself
So you think thin.
Eating to die
Is a fucking sin.
Chocolate orgasms are not on my agenda.
For sanity's sake
I've got to think slender.
Stuff it in
Pack it down
Cram cram cram
To know who I am.
Suppress my feelings with potatoes and bread
Food is filling my fucking head.
Creativity is what I want.
It comes from my hunger.
Find a space in my heart
To let it pulse
And I wonder
Why
This destructive urge
Purge yourself
So you think thin.
Breathe in the air.
Let it in.

Vanessa Whiteley

IN LIMBO

Turn in here at the main gate,
checking your watch for the time,
you're anxious not to be late,
unpunctuality's a crime.

A young man looks up. You enter.
He puts your name in the book.
You sit down in the very centre
and you both pretend not to look.

You sit musing ways of escape,
as your eyes gaze at the floor.
Your mind's on a dark landscape
and someone has opened the door.....

Ali Wade

ALI WAY IN HEAVEN

Anything that requires silence to be heard,
stillness to occur.
Anything that, with constant attention,
widens and deepens understanding.
Peeling off, and moving through, layers.
Exploring.
Knowing with each new discovery
that the awakening is for me, caused by the creator,
predating, purposefully at play,
aware of the pleasure in solving a mystery:

Any sculpture's shape my fingers can trace,
whose surface teaches my touch.
Any form that to my eye, informs, encircles and holds.
Anything that 'looking back', enjoys being looked at.
Anything I can wrap my mind's eye about,
the way I can wrap me, around you.

The joy these things give, and the joy you bring
is a feeling, communicated through, not living in,
the object. A communion between stillness and myself.
My own personal heaven, not a place, but an essence,
visited when in the presence of these things.
It is the very best of dreams and hopes,
a sense in which you are only a ghost,
haunting the heaven where joy resides.
I constantly seem to aspire
to a reminder
of tears.

Alyson Hallett

POEM 2

i want to go down
to the river in meself
it's what i want to do

i want to be there
in the river of meself
it's where i want to be

that river
deep, wide, unwinding
is me sexy
me sensual
me so completely free
ain't no-one
can stop me

moving

Jonathan Munn

JULIE

Hail to thee - young poetess
With smiling eyes, and golden hair.
Poets welcome you with pride
And know in you romance is never dead.

With your craft you will travel over lands;
Make love to handsome strangers, kiss and tell,
Traitors put to flight, tragedies unwind,
Criminals caught, infinities split.
(Or is that infinitives - I never am quite sure.)

And from your living room you can strike out
Against enemies, stand up to the foe.
Stab tyrants in the heart with pen and ink,
Protect the innocent, uphold the law.

Lose your virginity over again;
Or make love over a thousand miles.
Possibly invent your perfect mate
And make him do your bidding from the chair.

Do not fear your pen, it is your friend
And will light the way if it is dark.
You can bind the hearts of those who love you,
Carve yourself into the rock of life, then
History will hold you in its vice.

Rosemary Dun
DIFFERENCES

I have always
Believed
In integrity
But for you
It's just a
Word
That begins
With
The letter
I.

Bettina Sims-Hilditch

I SAW YOU
(The Delicatessen)

6.25 . . . number 23 . . .
"Greek salad for my tea"

6.26 . . . number 24 . . .
"Salami sausage, wild boar
freshest veal, bleeding rare
epicurean slaughter . . who cares
about animals . . give me more"

6.27 . . . number 23 . . .
"Who's this pig snorting behind me"

6.28 . . . number 24 . . .
"Sexy chick, do it on the floor
wiv 'er right now . . bet I could
pinch 'er arse,
no-one will see
I might just get lucky
tonight"

6.29 . . . number 25 . . .
sees the scene, gets the vibe
"Oi matey, I saw you
What do you think you're
do-
ing
That's my wife you're
insult-
ing"

6.30 . . . number 23 . . .
turns round to see
number 25 and number 24
scrapping on the floor

Turns on her heel
Raises her steel
Stiletto
Blows a kiss
Delivers a blow
Walks out of the door
Leaving number 24
Gasping for breath
Longing for death
and number 25
a VEGETARIAN.

Gary Cox

THE PORK CHOP PAGAN

I've gone from insane to sober
Sober to insane
I've tried to live without meat
But the story's just the same
I need pork
Beef, veal, lamb
I could eat a whole herd of cattle
Between two bread vans
I could eat venison, pheasant
Any type of game
Goose or grouse
Wild or tame
I could eat duck with orange
Apple with hare
Flambé sauté
Medium or rare

Do you care for a drink sir?
Yes, a pint of semen if you please
Don't forget the Bi-products
Just forget the BSE

Then you can eat the liver, the onions
The kidneys, the heart
You can eat the sweetbreads, the trotters
You can eat every part
Cos I hate the Veggies
And I hate the Vegans
This is Red Meat Religion
And I'm a **Pork Chop Pagan**

So when they've banned the red meat
And there is no more
I'll be dipping my bread
On the abattoir floor
Because I'm a carnivorous creep
With a point to make
Stuff the Vegetarians
And give me a steak!

Claire Berry

THIN

Cosmopolitan Woman
Perfect Woman
Thin, Thin and Thinner
Thin sells
Sex for the Thin
Beauty is Thin
Only desirable when a perfect Size 10
Magazines, posters, television
Thin is everywhere
Grab the flab
Cut it off
Or the world won't want you
No-one will want you
Woman equals Thin
Perfect lines
Perfect curves
Well I say

Flab is Funky
Flab is Woman
Flab is Beauty
Imperfect is Perfect

Goodbye to your message

Hello to Fat, to Flab
Embrace your Cellulite
Woman Round
Curvaceous
Pear-shaped
Cuddly
Wear what you like
Be who you like

COS FLAB IS FUNKY

Viva Imogen Hirst

CIDER

Cider makes the unbearable bearable.
Cider ends the distinction between the two.
Cider is the drink of those taken to the limits of endurance.
And, directly or indirectly, of their children also.

Cider is the drink of the rough and of the ready.
Cider is the drink of those who swing the pick and fork the hay.
Cider is the drink that makes these bearable.
And takes the awfulness of these away.

Somehow cider can bring understanding, wisdom.
Somehow cider reconciles the awfulness with the okay.
But even so, drinking it forever is not understanding.
Even so, drinking it forever is not okay.

Tôpher Mills

ALAS POOR YORRICKS

To don a condom, or not to don a condom,
                    that is the question:
Whether 'tis safer to don a condom and suffer
The pins and needles of outrageous genital cramp,
Or to boldly enter, unsheath-ed, a sea of HIV positives,
And by copulation disperse them? - To spread, - to carry:
Evermore; and, by this spread, thus we can end
The groin-ache, and the thousand unnatural perversions
That flesh is heir to, - 'tis a contamination
Recently to be fear'd. To lust, - to fuck; -
To fuck perchance to orgasm: - aye, there's the rub;
For in that fuck of fear what orgasms may
When we have struggled on that constrictive rubber,
Which must give us pause: there's the relaxant
That makes a calamity of such good sex;
For who can bear the slips for prolong-ed time,
The strangled dong, the pangs of imprisoned love,
The lust's delay, the insolence of rubber,
And the giggles that await it from some unworthy types,
When he himself might his quietus make
With a bare bodkin?
For whom would fardels bare, and for how much?
The uncover-ed penis, of whose spawn
No reveller admits, rubbers now fill,
And makes us rather bonk those we have had,
Than bonk with others we know not of?
Thus AIDS doth make cowards of us all;
And thus the native hue of copulation
Is sicklied o'er with the pale cast of sheath;
And enterprises of great lust and excit-e-ment,
With this regard, their moments turn awry,
And lose the name of PASSION!

Mike Gower

MATURER PEOPLE'S PARTIES

We wise drivers
drink only two plastic glasses
of tepid white wine.
The music, tasteful
non-intrusive, non-descript
is turned down
and there's lots of light too
to aid conversation
plenty of conversation
from plenty of people
in groups
not smoking
not dancing
not eating until the signal is given
not laughing much
no spillage on the floor
standing, talking
wearing our minds on our sleeves.

But there **were** parties
of dark lights
swirling smoke
and music crashing
through bodies
which shook and leapt
parties where booze
swilled and splashed
and fights erupted
like red hot lava
pouring through rooms
and down stairs

and everywhere people
and jeans and hands
and bodies embracing
and nakedness
and hot, dark noise.

But at **this** party
I doubt if anyone
will get laid.

Fran Jason

BLIND DATE

One day, on a walk in Paradise,
(otherwise known as O'Brien's Bridge)
I jokingly prayed for a little romance:
a man on a charger -
proverbial knight -
handsome & tall, devil-may-care:
Sure, I'd know him on sight.

While I sat by the river, the following day,
I'd had no idea, but I had been heard.
Though the message I'd sent
Had been garbled a bit (well, a lot, really)
True love came my way, on
That magical day.

A short man, in green, came over the hill,
patted my dog & offered me tea.
"Why not?" I thought.
"Seems harmless enough."
"Thank you," I said,
"Will you come & join me?"

And so began an adventure in love.
I was swept off my feet with surprise -
by the joy & the laughter,
by his touch & the look in his eyes.
No knight on white charger...
But oh! What charged nights!

Flo Kirk

SPOONS

We are a perfect match,
Like spoons we fit together,
I, nestled in the soft curve
Of your resting body,
Your chest against my back,
Knees against mine,
Your groin fitting neatly around my buttocks,
Nothing between our sweat-soaked bodies
But ourselves.

We are a perfect match,
Like spoons we fit together,
But spoons must not fit together too well
Lest they become one,
And in that melding one (at least) is lost,
So they remain separated
By a thin line of reality,
As we do - "for protection from ourselves".

We are a perfect match,
Like spoons we fit together,
And like spoons, we keep ourselves apart,
Just in case the expected separation hurts too much,
But the banyan tree is both separate and one,
Shared roots, shared lives makes the whole,
More than the sum of the many,
Maybe we should be like the banyan tree
And not like separate spoons,
Then the expected separation becomes impossible.

Claire Williamson

AND YOU

Me
and you
in bed
together
asleep

unconscious
of me
and you
in bed
together
asleep

I dream
a dream
I dream
of me
and you
in bed
together
asleep
and you
come to
make love
to me

I sleep
and you're
asleep

Later
you wake

and we
make love
and I
feel you
closer
to me
much more
than ever
before

We lie
together
bound by
our arms
and when
I breathe

    I breathe

    and you
    and you
    and you
    and you
    and you
    and you

Helen Blackburn

DESMOND MORRIS

Oh Desmond why do you do the things you do?
Does the Beeb dictate your partial view?

I have to make a quick confession
you ensnared me during my last depression.
It looked so logical I nearly agreed
that love's desire is the urge to breed
and romance is merely a continuous programme
to join our loins in fertile orgasm.

It's flavour of the month for you to say
that esoteric ponderings have had their day.
With your turtle neck and neat grey hair
you're a grinning mask of psychic despair.

Oh that it should come to this
just reduce us all to shit and piss.

A heap of convivial excrement
will be our only testament
to an evolving lateral consciousness
a global etheric magnificence.

Mr Morris go home and fuck your wife
and extrapolate your pair-bond if it justifies your life.

I thank you for your patronisation
for it rekindled my gross indignation
at the worthless dick-headed invasive assumption
that my sexual energy was born for your consumption.

I'm aroused by the rivers, mountains, trees
by the rustle in the hedgerows of yes, the birds and bees.

How dare you preach, how dare you say
that our capacity for love is just to make hay.

You're a fat fink, a petty dictator
a fashionable media-man's perpetrator
of the comforting hardcore western rule
inscribed by your flaccid boneless tool

to have and to hold, to trap and to own
the wet patch goes rancid once your seed has been sown.

Kevin McKeigue
The Lesbian and Gay Community

Has suffered far too long
But who out there can really judge
Say what is right, what is wrong
We blame them for spreading diseases
Educate yourselves - see if you can complain then
For these diseases are spread far more
By heterosexual women and men
I will never promote their lifestyle
But neither will I condemn
In my eyes I will treat them the same
As equal women and men
If everyone took this attitude
What a wonderful world it would be
No more discrimination
And only then could people be free

Stuart Butler (*The Stroud Football Poets*)

"COME AND BE A JUDGE
IF YOU THINK YOU'RE POSH ENOUGH"
(Or how to be a top judge).

First, be born white
And male.
Have a dad who is already
A top judge
And then go to Eton or Harrow;
Be posh,
Speak posh,
Be rich
And don't know who Paul Gascoigne is
And never hear of Oasis.
Believe that all black men are potential rapists
And that all women who wear short skirts
Want sexual intercourse with strangers.
Believe that animals like being hunted,
Hate trade unionists,
Think Tony Blair is a communist
And believe that wages are stolen profits.
Like wigs,
Like dressing up in a black cap
In the privacy of your own home
And like the 18th century
Criminal Code.
Like speaking Latin
And like playing with hammers,
But don't like carpenters.
Have 2 houses; with just one
In Gloucestershire.
Be a Mason,
But deny you are a Mason.

Never go on a bus;
Like cricket and rugby
But hate football.
Get married,
To a woman
(Must be white),
Ignore your wife
After having a son,
Then ignore him
By sending him
To Eton or Harrow.
And then continue the cycle
By returning to line 6.

Michelle Blower

THE CASHIER

Sliced white (beep)
Baked beans (beep)
Baked beans (beep)
"Smile it might never happen!"
False smile
Broccoli (beep)
Baked beans (beep)

Gazing over the shopping trolley of life:
The woman who always ties a yapping Jack Russell outside
And buys the cans of cheapest beer
Looks like a man in drag.

"Don't squash the buns and make sure the trifles are upright,"
Red face, white hair. He hostiley pushes his whingeing mother's wheelchair.
"Do you want to do it yourself?" he juxtaposes the trifles between
the quiche and the crisps.
He laughs to the disinterested general public.
I know and he knows that he is annoyed.
Veins protrude from his neck as he laughs.
A baby stares from a pram.
We are all dependent on one another.
The whingeing mother is wrapped up in gloves and blanket in the wheelchair.

Here, sitting at the cognitive cash-till,
They are buying a part of me,
Tinned toms (beep)
Tinned toms (beep)
Razors x 4 (beep)
Brain (beep)
Ego (beep)

Outside, last night, one tramp stabbed another,
The homeless drunk now a murderer
Whilst his dead friend's ghost chills me. Kill me.

"Aren't you cold sat there?" is another pensioner's
Rusty rhetoric,
The hang-dog sad-dog floppy-faced farmer
Apologetically buys cider.

The man that used to work here and collect the baskets has gone mad.
He stands around the cashier area pointing and talking nonsense.
Everyone pretends that he's not really here. After all he used to collect the
baskets, he's not dangerous.
He's not really here, until, "it's a shame," acknowledges the woman in the
queue, "he used to work here and collect the baskets."
"Maybe that's why he still comes here," I offer.
"It's a shame," she repeats and looks for support. But I just think he's weird.

They shop,
Secretly crying soap powder tears
And soap opera fears drip, drip, drip
A mundane depression onto my frown,
Spaghetti (beep)
Carrots (beep)
Catfood (beep)
Catfood (beep)
Catfood (beep)
Baked beans (beep)

"How much is the celery?"
The sss from 'celery' whistles suppressed aggression through my teeth
and into the self-important intercom.
"Smile it might never happen!"
Aggression, suppressed, flows around and into shaking cashier's hands
Pressing the wrong button
Jamming the till
(BEEEEEEPPPPP!!!!!!)
A staring queue evolves,
An overring, an oversight,
As Ashmir the bearded beetle
Scuttles from his rock
("Remember Ashmir is the <u>BOSS</u>" - 'boss' underlined and hung on the
chilly stockroom wall)

"it's just an overring," I explain,
Like the overring of life,
I've been charged too much,
Tinned toms (beep)
Small granary (beep)
Tinned toms (beep)
Catfood (beep).

Daniel Cassiel

THE LOTTERY OF LOVE

I bought my ticket on Saturday night
At 7.29.
You said you were my bonus number.

8.05 and I said "Fuck it."
Anthea had not released my balls.

Next week I tried a different combination,
Based on my tortoise's birthday.

Six whole days I dreamed:
Of buying a Ferrari -
Not with petrol, just that we could shag in;

Of giving young children transplants
Whether they needed them or not,
Just so you knew I cared;

Of taking us on holiday
To Paris or Jamaica
To meet the couples off 'Blind Date'.

But now you've run off
With an unemployed carpet-fitter from Selkirk
Whose name begins with S,
Exactly as Mystic Meg said you would.
(He is watching with his mother.
His pigeons have the mange).

I don't agree with the lottery on principle.

But -
You scratch my card, I'll scratch yours.

Peter Wyton

UNDER THE STAIRS

The mat in the hall holds a mountain of envelopes,
Tax bills and final demands,
Writs and subpoenas and breath test results,
So I sit with my head in my hands
Where it's cosy and dark and there's no-one to shout,
I'm under the stairs and I'm not coming out.

My mistress arrived on the doorstep at dawn
With a carrycot under her arm,
My wife, who had not met my mistress before,
Exhibited signs of alarm,
I can still hear the ongoing wrestling bout,
But I'm under the stairs and I'm not coming out.

My son's been a criminal genius from birth,
He was weaned upon steroids and liquor,
At his Christening service he half-inched the font
And stubbed out his fag on the vicar.
Now he's up in his cot with a gallon of stout
And I'm under the stairs and I'm not coming out.

There's an archangel perched on my satellite dish,
The devil's defrosting the fridge,
Salman Rushdie, my granny, Lord Lucan and Shergar
Are up in the loft playing bridge,
A bailiff's impaled on my rottweiler's snout,
But I'm under the stairs and I'm not coming out.

Alexander Grant

JESSE JAMES RIDES INTO TOWN ON A POGO STICK

Boing
Boing
Boing
Boing
Boing
Boing
BANG!

Glenn Carmichael

PIMPS OF THE ALPHABET

Every poet I ever knew was a cripple.
Now, maybe that's just because everybody is a cripple in some way or other.
But I say, "Poets, throw away your crutches, and walk to me, walk to me.
Talk to me, talk to me."

Hey, what are we,
Wimps or what?
No we're not,
We're pimps!

Words,
Use them and abuse them,
Put them out on the street
To make you some money.

Some of the best people I ever knew
Were pimps.
Some of the best people I know
Are pimps,
They're pimps of the alphabet.

So tell me pretty porkies,
Pretty jackanories.
As long as it's good,
I don't care if it's true.
Fiction or non-fiction,
It doesn't matter to me.
It doesn't have to be the truth,
Just the way that it should be.

"Ooh baby, I'm sorry I hurt you,
I really didn't mean to,
But you asked for the truth,

And so that's what I told you."

Don't think about it,
Feel it!
Don't give them what they want,
Make them need it...
On their knees
Bleeding for it.
Cos we're the pushers,
They're the junkies.
You want some more?
OK, well show me your money.
OK, give me a deposit
And I'll give you a taste,
But don't make empty promises
I ain't got time to waste.
Don't even think that I wrote
These words for you.
If you don't want them
There's others who do.

I'm sorry if this poem isn't quite right,
But don't worry about that
I can do you a re-write.
I'll change it around,
So the black bits are white.
I'll change the perfume,
So it smells like shite.
I'll get a new broom,
Sweep it all out of sight.
Anything...
Anything I can do to please.
I'll juggle those words
With the greatest of ease.
I'll cross all the i's,
And I'll dot all the t's.

Because we're...

Pimps of the alphabet,
Selling satisfaction.
A really good time,
Or a little distraction.
Getting our share
Of a piece of the action.
Fact or Fict
Fict or Faction.
We want words
Out on the street
Doin' the hustle,
Not lying in traction
Pulling a muscle.

Words, words, words,
Use 'em and abuse 'em.
Send them out workin'.
Send them out cruisin'.
Send them out fightin'
For a bit of a bruisin'.
Write words to win
Cos there's no point in losin'.

Words, words, words
Are guns loaded with meaning.
Shoot them at the heart
Leave 'em buggered and bleeding.
Send 'em out rockin',
Rockin' and a reelin'.
Make 'em do the jive,
Make 'em dance on the ceiling.

Pimps of the alphabet,
Yee-ha!

Pimps of the alphabet,
Sha-na-na-na-na.
Pimps of the alphabet,
Bee-bop-a-loo-la.
Pimps of the alphabet,
Shoo-be-doo-be-doo-bah.

Ring-a-ling-ding,
Every word ringing true.
Yes, we're pimps of the alphabet,
So make words work
                    for you.

PIMP$ of the ALPHAB£T

Formed in 1995.
One aim:
to make words work
for you.

…an Carmichael & Sara-Jane Arbury

THANK YOU FOR READING THIS BOOK

It was brought into being with determination, hard work and the support and love of all the contributing poets. PotA would particularly like to express sincere gratitude to The Bristol Poetry Slam, Gingha Inc. and all those who donated money at benefit gigs, Adam Horovitz (Hoo-Hah), Arnolfini Bookshop, The Poetry Can and *strangefish*.

If you have any comments about The Bristol Slam Poetry Anthology and/or would like information on any of the poets featured, please write (enclosing a stamped addressed envelope) to:

PotA
130c Lower Cheltenham Place
Montpelier
Bristol
BS6 5LF

PUBLICATIONS BY PIMP$ of the ALPHAB£T PRESS

The Truth Is Optional (ISBN 0-9526432-0-0) - Glenn Carmichael.
£4.99 + £1.00 p&p.

Gutted (ISBN 0-9526432-1-9) - Sara-Jane Arbury.
£1.95 + 50p p&p.

Blind Peeping (ISBN 0-9526432-2-7) - Claire Williamson.
£1.95 + 50p p&p.

Postscript Poems (ISBN 0-9526432-3-5) - Gary Cox.
£1.95 + 50p p&p.

Order direct from PotA at the above address.

INDEX